Preface

Singapore Math® Intensive Practice is a series of 12 b... ...g supplementary material for Singapore math programs.

The primary objective of this series of books is to help students generate greater interest in mathematics and gain more confidence in solving mathematical problems. To achieve this, special features are incorporated in the series.

SPECIAL FEATURES

Topical Review

Enables students of mixed abilities to be exposed to a good variety of questions which are of varying levels of difficulty so as to help them develop a better understanding of mathematical concepts and their applications.

Mid-Year or End-Of-Year Review

Provides students with a good review that summarizes the topics learned in Singapore math programs.

Take the Challenge!

Deepens students' mathematical concepts and helps develop their mathematical reasoning and higher-order thinking skills as they practice their problem-solving strategies.

More Challenging Problems

Stimulate students' interest through challenging and thought-provoking problems which encourage them to think critically and creatively as they apply their knowledge and experience in solving these problems.

Why this Series?

Students will find this series of books a good complement and supplement to Singapore math programs. The comprehensive coverage certainly makes this series a valuable resource for teachers, parents and tutors.

It is hoped that the special features in this series of books will inspire and spur young people to achieve better mathematical competency and greater mathematics problem-solving skills.

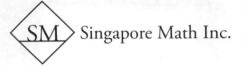

Singapore Math Inc.

Published by
Singapore Math Inc.
19535 SW 129th Ave.
Tualatin, OR 97062
U.S.A.
E-mail: customerservice@singaporemath.com
www.singaporemath.com

First published 2004
Reprinted 2005, 2007, 2008, 2009, 2010, 2011,
2013, 2014, 2015, 2017, 2018, 2019, 2020

Singapore Math® Intensive Practice 5A
ISBN 978-1-932906-08-0

Printed in China

Our special thanks to Jenny Kempe for her assistance in editing
Singapore Math® Intensive Practice.

Intensive Practice 5A
Contents

Topic 1: Whole Numbers

1. Write the following numerals in words.

   (a) 6037

   Six thousand, thirty - seven

   (b) 89,023

   Eight nine thousand, twenty three

   (c) 999,999

   Nine hundred ninety - nine thousand, nine hundred ninety nine

   (d) 305,010

   Three hundred five thousand, ten

   (e) 3,946,238

   Three million nine hundred forty six thousand, two hundred thirty eight

   (f) 240,527

   Two hundred forty thousand, five hundre twenty seven.

2. Write the following in numerals.

   (a) Nine thousand, twelve — _9,012_

   (b) Seventy-six thousand, five hundred thirty-nine — _76,539_

   (c) One hundred thousand, one hundred — _100,100_

   (d) One million, one hundred thousand, ten — _1,100,010_

   (e) Two hundred twenty-four thousand, fifteen — _224,015_

   (f) Three million, thirty-one thousand, eighty-four — _3,031,084_

3. Fill in the blanks

(a) The digit '7' is in the _hundreds_ place of the number 62,718.

(b) The digit '___2___' is in the thousands place of the number 352,806.

(c) The digit '3' stands for ___3___ in the numeral 100,003.

(d) The place value of the digit '9' in the numeral 216,497 is _tens_.

(e) The value of the digit '2' in the numeral 4,216,909 is _200,000_.

(f) The value of the digit '___1___' in the number 524,132 is 100.

(g) In the numeral 291,609, the digit '9' is in both the _ones_ and the _Ten thousands_ places.

(h) In 840,365, the digit '8' stands for 8 × _100,000_.

4. Arrange the numbers in increasing order.

(a) 16,273 ; 16,349 ; 12,372 ; 13,673
    (3)   (4)   (1)   (2)

_12,372 ~ 13,673 ~ 16,273 ~ 16,349_

(b) 83,900 ; 38,090 ; 19,032 ; 19,302
    (4)   (3)   (1)   (2)

_19,032 ~ 19,302 ~ 38,090 ~ 83,900_

5. Arrange the numbers in decreasing order.

(a) 96,669 ; 69,696 ; 99,669 ; 69,669
    (2)   (3)   (1)   (4)

_99,669 ~ 96,669 ~ 69,696 ~ 69,669_

(b) 25,225 ; 55,255 ; 55,552 ; 25,252
    (4)   (2)   (1)   (3)

_55,552 ~ 55,255 ~ 25,252 ~ 25,225_

6. (a) Which is greater, (32,168) or 23,861?   _32,168_

   (b) Which is smaller, 94,560 or (91,560?)   _91,560_

   (c) Which is the largest, 56,370, 56,307 or (57,307?)   _57,307_

   (d) Which is the smallest, 108,321, (108,123) or 109,132?   _108,123_

7. **7 1 8 4 7**

Rearrange all the digits to make

   (a)   the largest possible number,   8 7, 7⁴11

   (b)   the smallest possible number,   14, 7 7 8

   (c)   the smallest possible **odd** number,   14, 787

   (d)   the largest possible **even** number.   8 7, 714

8. **6 1 0 9 2 3 4**

Rearrange all the digits to make

   (a)   the largest possible number,   9,643,210

   (b)   the smallest possible number,   1,023,469

   (c)   the largest possible **odd** number,   9,643,201

   (d)   the smallest possible **even** number.   1,023,496

9. (a)   There are   234,489   ones in the number 234,489.

   (b)   There are   3,442   hundreds in the number 344,298.

   (c)   In the numeral 3,000,000, there are   3,000   thousands.

   (d)   The number 621,540 has   62   ten thousands.

   (e)   In the numeral 1,472,583, there are   14,725   hundreds.

   (f)   The number 796,001 has   79,600   tens.

10. Fill in the blanks.

   (a) $240,579 = 200,000 + $ 40,000 $+ 500 + 79$

   (b) $142,339 = 140,000 + $ 2,000 $+ 39$

   (c) $603,714 = $ 100,000 $+ 503,714$

   (d) $635,759 = 630,059 + $ 5,700

   (e) $1,234,567 = 1,002,507 + $ 232,060

   (f) $5,862,936 = $ 62,036 $+ 5,800,900$

11. Fill in the blanks.

    (a)   52,273 is 100 more than ____52,373____ .

    (b)   73,857 is ____100____ more than 73,757.

    (c)   ____37,099____ is 100 more than 36,999.

    (d)   82,383 is 1000 more than ____81,383____ .

    (e)   30,094 is ____100____ more than 29,994.

    (f)   ____38,429____ is 1000 more than 37,429.

    (g)   78,489 is 1000 more than ____77,439____ .

    (h)   ____38,686____ is 10,000 more than 28,686.

    (i)   56,145 is 10,000 more than ____46,145____ .

    (j)   ____601,466____ is 100,000 more than 501,466.

12. Fill in the blanks.

    (a)   47,272 is 100 less than ____47,372____ .

    (b)   90,765 is ____100____ less than 90,865.

    (c)   ____53,484____ is 100 less than 53,584.

    (d)   47,613 is 1000 less than ____48,613____ .

    (e)   31,990 is ____100____ less than 32,090.

    (f)   ____75,245____ is 1000 less than 76,245.

    (g)   90,778 is 1000 less than ____91,778____ .

    (h)   ____23,421____ is 10,000 less than 33,421.

    (i)   25,613 is 10,000 less than ____35,613____ .

    (j)   ____537,011____ is 100,000 less than 637,011.

13. Round off the following numbers to the nearest ten.

    (a)   4   ____0____   (b)   5   ____10____

    (c)   46   ____50____   (d)   803   ____800____

    (e)   7309   ____7310____   (f)   20,002   ____20,000____

(g) 67,499 _67,500_ (h) 98,999 _99,000_

(i) 43,296 _43,300_ (j) 7920 _7,920_

(k) 348 _350_ (l) 70,624 _70,620_

14. Round off the following numbers to the nearest hundred.

   (a) 49 _0_ (b) 87 _100_

   (c) 265 _300_ (d) 904 _900_

   (e) 3419 _3400_ (f) 40,050 _40,100_

   (g) 73,945 _73,900_ (h) 9521 _9,500_

   (i) 863 _900_ (j) 6997 _7,000_

   (k) 8500 _8500_ (l) 99,501 _99,500_

15. Round off the following numbers to the nearest thousand.

   (a) 498 _0_ (b) 630 _1000_

   (c) 959 _1000_ (d) 1600 _2000_

   (e) 2769 _3000_ (f) 49,490 _49,500_

   (g) 3094 _3000_ (h) 7562 _8000_

   (i) 6303 _6000_ (j) 9597 _10,000_

   (k) 73,210 _73,000_ (l) 299,513 _300,000_

16. The following numbers have been rounded off to the nearest ten. What are the smallest and greatest possible numbers they could have been?

	Estimated number	Smallest possible actual number	Greatest possible actual number
(a)	70	64	74
(b)	390	385	394
(c)	6000	5995	6004
(d)	73,000	72995	73,004

5

17. The following numbers have been rounded off to the nearest hundred. What are the smallest and greatest possible numbers they could have been?

	Estimated number	Smallest possible actual number	Greatest possible actual number
(a)	300	250	349
(b)	7500	7456	7549
(c)	10,000	9950	10,049
(d)	47,700	47,650	47,749

18. The following numbers have been rounded off to the nearest thousand. What are the smallest and greatest possible numbers they could have been?

	Estimated number	Smallest possible actual number	Greatest possible actual number
(a)	1000	500	1499
(b)	6000	5500	7549
(c)	35,000	34500	35.499
(d)	91,000	90,500	91499

19. (a) 2345 kg is _____ when rounded off to the nearest ten kilograms and _____ when rounded off to the nearest hundred kilograms.

(b) $35,678 is _____ when rounded off to the nearest ten dollars and _____ when rounded off to the nearest thousand dollars.

(c) 390,035 m is _____ when rounded off to the nearest hundred meters and _____ when rounded off to the nearest thousand meters.

(d) 795,299 ml is _____ when rounded off to the nearest ten milliliters and _____ when rounded off to the nearest thousand milliliters.

20. Round off each number and then estimate the value of

    (a) $38 + 719 \approx$ $40 + 700 = 740$ (b) $346 + 659 \approx$ $300 + 700 = 1000$

    (c) $1042 + 6382 \approx$ $1000 + 6000 = 7600$ (d) $7412 + 12{,}023 \approx$ $7000 + 12{,}000 = 19{,}000$

    (e) $13{,}979 + 23{,}200 \approx$ $14{,}000 + 23{,}000 = 37{,}000$ (f) $47{,}168 + 8985 \approx$ $47000 + 9000 = 56000$

    (g) $67{,}104 + 70{,}905 \approx$ $67{,}000 + 71{,}000 = 138{,}000$ (h) $93{,}206 + 81{,}047 \approx$ $93000 + 81000 = 174000$

21. Round off each number and then estimate the value of

    (a) $913 - 79 \approx$ 800 (b) $867 - 387 \approx$ 500

    (c) $1005 - 682 \approx$ 300 (d) $3443 - 1203 \approx$ 2000

    (e) $7758 - 2081 \approx$ 6000 (f) $10{,}986 - 8029 \approx$ 3000

    (g) $45{,}964 - 22{,}213 \approx$ $24{,}000$ (h) $89{,}006 - 61{,}794 \approx$ 27000

22. Estimate the value of

    (a) $89 \times 7 \approx$ 630 (b) $162 \times 8 \approx$ 1600

    (c) $1735 \times 6 \approx$ 12000 (d) $6209 \times 5 \approx$ 30000

    (e) $713 \times 8 \approx$ 5600 (f) $1986 \times 9 \approx$ 18000

    (g) $9 \times 798 \approx$ 7200 (h) $61{,}856 \times 4 \approx$ 248000

23. Estimate the value of

    (a) $97 \div 8 \approx$ 12 (b) $421 \div 6 \approx$ 70

    (c) $3835 \div 5 \approx$ 800 (d) $8888 \div 9 \approx$ 1000

    (e) $1328 \div 3 \approx$ 400 (f) $586 \div 4 \approx$ 150

    (g) $40{,}298 \div 8 \approx$ 5000 (h) $73{,}208 \div 7 \approx$ $10{,}000$

24. Work out these problems.

    (a) House A, B and C have floor areas of 2489 m^2, 3234 m^2 and 6071 m^2 respectively. Estimate the total floor area of the three houses.

(b)   In 2000, the population of a town, Burgundy, was 44,756. In 2001, the population had risen by 9873. Find the population of Burgundy in 2001 and round it off to the nearest thousand.

25. Multiply.

(a) $26 \times 10 =$ 260

(b) $794 \times 10 =$ 7940

(c) $1426 \times 10 =$ 14260

(d) $7200 \times 50 =$ 360,000

(e) $3210 \times 40 =$ 128,400

(f) $624 \times 70 =$ 43,680

26. Multiply.

(a) $68 \times 100 =$ 6800

(b) $404 \times 200 =$ 80,800

(c) $1536 \times 100 =$ 133,600

(d) $615 \times 300 =$ 184,500

(e) $1200 \times 700 =$ 840,000

(f) $3600 \times 600 =$ 2,160,000

27. Multiply.

(a) $54 \times 1000 =$ 54,000

(b) $49 \times 2000 =$ 98,000

(c) $531 \times 1000 =$ 531,000

(d) $610 \times 5000 =$ 3,050,000

(e) $105 \times 8000 =$ 840,000

(f) $960 \times 6000 =$ 5,760,000

28. Estimate the value of each of the following.

(a) $36 \times 149 \approx$ 6000

(b) $634 \times 790 \approx$ 480,000

(c) $3248 \times 519 \approx$ 1,500,000

(d) $62 \times 805 \approx$ 48000

(e) $2417 \times 48 \approx$ 100,000

(f) $2903 \times 68 \approx$ 210,000

29. Work out these problems.

(a)   Mr. Yap ordered two and a half dozen television sets. If each set cost $980, how much did he have to pay? Give your answer to the nearest thousand dollars.

980 × 30 = 24 400 ≈ 29 000

8

6/29

(b) Mrs. Sweet sells 151 pieces of candy each day. Give an estimate of the total number of pieces of candy she will sell in 3 weeks.

$200 \times 3 = 600$

(c) At a carnival, there are 117 stalls. If each stall makes a profit of $485 a day, about how much profit will all the stalls make in a day?

30. Divide.

(a) $60 \div 10 =$ 6

(b) $940 \div 10 =$ 94

(c) $1650 \div 10 =$ 165

(d) $8400 \div 60 =$ 140

(e) $3600 \div 90 =$ 400

(f) $6370 \div 70 =$ 91

31. Divide.

(a) $800 \div 100 =$ 8

(b) $4500 \div 500 =$ 9

(c) $1500 \div 100 =$ 15

(d) $9600 \div 800 =$ 12

(e) $10,500 \div 300 =$ 35

(f) $28,800 \div 400 =$ 72

32. Divide.

(a) $54,000 \div 1000 =$ 54

(b) $92,000 \div 2000 =$ 46

(c) $50,000 \div 1000 =$ 50

(d) $48,000 \div 6000 =$ 8

(e) $120,000 \div 5000 =$ 24

(f) $450,000 \div 9000 =$ 50

33. Estimate the value of each of the following.

(a) $263 \div 27 \approx$ 10

(b) $1634 \div 78 \approx$ 20

(c) $804 \div 19 \approx$ 40

(d) $5520 \div 53 \approx$ 120

(e) $21,948 \div 29 \approx$ 700

(f) $12,903 \div 37 \approx$ 300

34. Work out these problems.

(a) A tank with a capacity of 23,795 cm^3 is completely filled with water. All the water is to be poured into small containers with a capacity of 745 cm^3 each. Estimate the number of small containers needed.

(b) Mr. Singh sold 595 curry puffs in a month. Estimate the total number of curry puffs he sold in a week. (Take 1 month = 4 weeks)

$600 \times 4 = 2400$

(c) Harry took up a bank loan of $47,900 which is inclusive of interest. He had to pay monthly installments of $820 to the bank. Give an estimate of the number of months needed to repay the full loan.

35. Find the value of

(a) $26 + 43 - 19 =$ 50

(b) $79 - 48 + 67 =$ 98

(c) $63 - 13 - 10 =$ 40

(d) $101 - 34 + 25 =$ 92

(e) $41 + 47 - 27 =$ 61

(f) $62 + 23 + 89 =$ 174

36. Find the value of

(a) $8 \times 7 \times 3 =$ 168

(b) $4 \times 9 \times 6 =$ 216

(c) $8 \times 6 \div 12 =$ 4

(d) $81 \div 9 \div 3 =$ 3

(e) $12 \times 7 \div 3 =$ 28

(f) $72 \div 24 \times 14 =$ 42

37. Find the value of

(a) $7 + 9 \times 3 =$ 34

(b) $48 \div 6 - 5 =$ 3

(c) $8 \times 7 + 46 =$ 102

(d) $49 + 15 \div 5 =$ 52

(e) $16 \times 10 - 68 =$ 92

(f) $108 \div 12 + 13 =$ 22

10

38. Find the value of

$\begin{array}{ll} \text{(a)} & 5 \times 9 + 56 \div 8 = \quad 52 \end{array}$

(a) $5 \times 9 + 56 \div 8 = \quad 52$

(b) $81 \div 9 - 5 + 7 =$

(c) $16 + 64 \div 4 \times 7 = \quad 128$

(d) $12 \div 3 \times 8 - 30 + 2 =$

(e) $3 \times 6 - 65 \div 5 = \quad 5$

(f) $34 - 7 \times 4 \div 14 =$

(g) $100 - 7 \times 42 \div 3 + 12 =$

(h) $17 + 54 \div 6 - 4 \times 5 =$

39. Find the value of

(a) $6 \times (4 + 7) =$

(b) $77 \div (23 - 12) =$

(c) $(6 \times 7) \div 2 + 29 =$

(d) $100 \div (17 + 3) - 5 =$

(e) $(93 - 76) \times 2 - 18 \div 3 =$

(f) $320 - (7 \times 30) \div 5 + 45 =$

(g) $144 \div 12 \times (4 + 2) - 34 =$

(h) $12 \times (15 - 8) \div 6 =$

40. What is the missing number in each box?

(a) $17 \times 9 + (\boxed{} \div 3) - 12 \times 2 = 138$

(b) $720 - \boxed{} \times 81 + 28 = 100$

41. I am thinking of some numbers. Examine the given clues and work backwards to find the numbers that I am thinking of.

(a)   If you add 6 to the number and then halve the result, you will get 8.

(b)   If you multiply the number by 9 and then add 3 to the result, you will get 75.

(c)   If you subtract 5 from the number and then double the result, you will get 40.

(d)   If you triple the number and subtract 4 from the result, you will get 80.

42. Insert the signs of operations to make each of the following number sentences correct.

Example: $(5 + 5 - 5) \div 5 = 1$

(a) $5 \ \boxed{} \ 5 \ \boxed{} \ 5 \ \boxed{} \ 5 = 25$

(b) $5 \ \boxed{} \ 5 \ \boxed{} \ 5 \ \boxed{} \ 5 = 0$

11

43. In each of the following, use any three of the numbers, **3, 4, 5, 12** and **15**, to make a correct number sentence. Each number can only be used **once** in each case.

Example: $12 - (15 \div 3) = 7$

(a) $\boxed{} \times \boxed{} + \boxed{} = 23$

(b) $(\boxed{} - \boxed{}) \div \boxed{} = 1$

(c) $\boxed{} - (\boxed{} \div \boxed{}) = 9$

(d) $(\boxed{} + \boxed{}) \times \boxed{} = 27$

44. You are given four cards as shown.

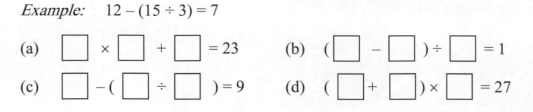

| 3 | 5 | 7 | 8 |

(a) How many different 4-digit even numbers can you form?

(b) How many different 4-digit odd numbers can you form?

(c) How many different 3-digit numbers, that are divisible by 3, can you form?

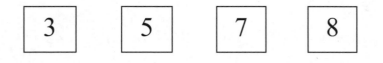

WORD PROBLEMS

1. Josh saves 75 cents of his allowance daily. How much will he save in one month? (Take 1 month = 30 days)
Give your answer to the nearest dollars.

2. A man bought a living room furniture set. He paid a deposit and the balance of $1499 was paid by monthly installments for one year. Estimate the amount of money he paid each month.

3. A bottle can hold 450 ml of milk. How many such bottles are required to hold 8.8 liters of milk? (1 liter = 1000 ml)

4. A coat costs $105. It costs 3 times as much as a sweater. Find the cost of 3 coats and 5 sweaters.

5. Jack's monthly salary is $1850. He gives his wife half of his monthly salary, spends $348 on himself and saves the rest. If he saves the same amount each month, how much will he save in a year? Give your answer to the nearest thousand dollars.

6. Jamal caught 8 more grasshoppers than spiders for his science project. A grasshopper has 6 legs and a spider has 8 legs. He counted a total of 188 legs. How many spiders and grasshoppers did he catch?

7. A shopkeeper had 1080 apples and oranges altogether. After selling 60 oranges, the number of apples he had was three times the number of oranges left. How many oranges did he have at first?

8. Dominic has twice as many peanuts as Leo. How many peanuts must Dominic give Leo so that each of them have 288 peanuts?

9. Dahlia paid $216 for 4 blouses and 5 skirts. A skirt cost 4 times as much as a blouse. How much did Dahlia pay for the 5 skirts?

10. Tim and Shelley have a total of 3450 coins in their piggy banks. Shelley and Nina have a total of 5130 coins. Nina has 5 times as many coins as Tim. How many coins does Shelley have?

11. Nicholas collects three times as many coins as William. Yasmin collects 21 coins less than Nicholas. The 3 children collect a total of 427 coins. How many coins does Yasmin have?

12. Katy is 16 years younger than Tess. Nina is 8 years older than Katy. The sum of their ages is 189. Find the age of each lady.

13. Andy and Barry saved a total of $368. Cindy and Daisy saved a total of $246. Andy and Daisy had the same amount of savings, while Barry saved 5 times as much as Cindy. How much savings did each person have?

14. The price of tickets for a musical is as follows:

Adult	$54
Child	$36

30 more adult tickets than child tickets were sold at the end of a certain day. If a total of $9000 was collected for that day, how many adults and children attended the musical?

15. A big bottle of olive oil cost $12 and a small bottle of olive oil cost $8. Thirty bottles of olive oil were sold for a total of $264. How many small bottles of olive oil were sold if there were more small bottles than big bottles sold? (Hint: Use the 'Guess and Check' method.)

Take the Challenge!

1. Use the digit '8' eight times to form five numbers which add up to 1000. Fill in the numbers in the boxes.

$$\boxed{} + \boxed{} + \boxed{} + \boxed{} + \boxed{} = 1000$$

2. Study the pattern. What is the missing number in the mouth of the last mask?

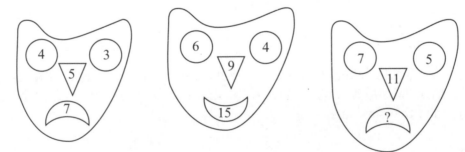

3. Use signs of operations to form an expression
   (a) with 6 nines to give a value of 100,
   (b) with 6 sevens to give a value of 110.

4. In each of the following **Cryptarithms**, each of the different letters represents a different single-digit number. The first letter of each word does not represent the number zero. Deduce the number represented by each letter.

   (a)   S E N D   (b)   U S E

       +   M O R E   +   L E S S

            M O N E Y   K I D D Y

   (c)   A D A M

             A N D

       +   E V E

          M O V E D

5. If you write down all the numbers from 1 to 100, how many times would you write the digit '3' ?

6. A worm is at the bottom of a jar that is 30 cm deep. Each day the worm crawls up 3 cm, but it slides down 2 cm at night. At this rate, how many days will the worm take to crawl out of the jar?

17

Topic 2: Multiplication and Division by a 2-digit Whole Number

1. Multiply.

   (a) $\begin{array}{r} 67 \\ \times\ 50 \\ \hline \\ \hline \end{array}$ (b) $\begin{array}{r} 43 \\ \times\ 70 \\ \hline \\ \hline \end{array}$ (c) $\begin{array}{r} 61 \\ \times\ 60 \\ \hline \\ \hline \end{array}$

   (d) $\begin{array}{r} 782 \\ \times\ 40 \\ \hline \\ \hline \end{array}$ (e) $\begin{array}{r} 409 \\ \times\ 80 \\ \hline \\ \hline \end{array}$ (f) $\begin{array}{r} 356 \\ \times\ 90 \\ \hline \\ \hline \end{array}$

   (g) $\begin{array}{r} 7084 \\ \times\ 30 \\ \hline \\ \hline \end{array}$ (h) $\begin{array}{r} 8006 \\ \times\ 50 \\ \hline \\ \hline \end{array}$ (i) $\begin{array}{r} 3447 \\ \times\ 20 \\ \hline \\ \hline \end{array}$

2. Multiply.

   (a) $\begin{array}{r} 34 \\ \times\ 35 \\ \hline \\ \hline \end{array}$ (b) $\begin{array}{r} 56 \\ \times\ 68 \\ \hline \\ \hline \end{array}$ (c) $\begin{array}{r} 314 \\ \times\ 47 \\ \hline \\ \hline \end{array}$

   (d) $\begin{array}{r} 1035 \\ \times\ 53 \\ \hline \\ \hline \end{array}$ (e) $\begin{array}{r} 523 \\ \times\ 38 \\ \hline \\ \hline \end{array}$ (f) $\begin{array}{r} 2133 \\ \times\ 69 \\ \hline \\ \hline \end{array}$

3. Multiply.

   (a) $39 \times 49 =$ (b) $87 \times 23 =$

   (c) $526 \times 35 =$ (d) $378 \times 64 =$

   (e) $1094 \times 24 =$ (f) $7654 \times 53 =$

   (g) $3801 \times 86 =$ (h) $5143 \times 95 =$

4. Divide.

(a) $20 \overline{\smash{)}\ 84}$ (b) $31 \overline{\smash{)}\ 76}$

(c) $40 \overline{\smash{)}\ 416}$ (d) $52 \overline{\smash{)}\ 267}$

(e) $80 \overline{\smash{)}\ 789}$ (f) $67 \overline{\smash{)}\ 499}$

(g) $24 \overline{\smash{)}\ 9240}$ (h) $76 \overline{\smash{)}\ 7709}$

5. Find the quotient and the remainder.

(a) $117 \div 26 =$ (b) $270 \div 15 =$

(c) $987 \div 28 =$ (d) $864 \div 36 =$

(e) $3612 \div 75 =$ (f) $9608 \div 32 =$

(g) $3876 \div 48 =$ (h) $6001 \div 98 =$

6. Look at the following example:

13×54
$= 13 \times (50 + 4)$
$= 13 \times 50 + 13 \times 4$
$= 650 + 52$
$= 702$

Note: $\square \times (\bigcirc + \triangle) = \square \times \bigcirc + \square \times \triangle$

Using the method shown in the example, do the following.

(a) $39 \times 42 =$ (b) $67 \times 23 =$

(c) $35 \times 39 =$ (d) $42 \times 54 =$

(e) $125 \times 24 =$ (f) $78 \times 62 =$

(g) $316 \times 41 =$ (h) $403 \times 93 =$

(i)   Find the cost of 16 boxes of chocolate if each box costs $1.05.

7. Look at the following example:

13×49
$= 13 \times (50 - 1)$
$= 13 \times 50 - 13 \times 1$
$= 650 - 13$
$= 637$

Note: $\square \times (\bigcirc - \triangle) = \square \times \bigcirc - \square \times \triangle$

Using the method shown in the example, do the following.

(a) $39 \times 49 =$ (b) $67 \times 39 =$

(c) $45 \times 27 =$ (d) $52 \times 58 =$

(e) $125 \times 19 =$ (f) $89 \times 67 =$

(g) $316 \times 68 =$ (h) $615 \times 99 =$

(i)   Find the product of 56 and 199.

8. In each of the following, what digit does each star represent?

(a)
```
       3 5
  ×  ★ ★
  ───────
     ★ ★
   ★ ★
  ───────
   7 7 0
  ───────
```

(b)
```
       7 8
  ×  ★ ★
  ───────
     ★ ★
   ★ ★ ★
  ───────
   4 7 5 8
  ───────
```

(c)
```
     ★ ★
  ×  ★ ★
  ───────
     8 ★
   ★ 4
  ───────
   4 2 5
  ───────
```

(d)
$$7 \overline{) \, \star \; 9 \; \star} \quad \text{(quotient } \star \, 4 \, \star)$$

(e)
$$6 \overline{) \, \star \; \star \; 2} \quad \text{(quotient } 9 \, \star)$$

(f)
$$\star \, 2 \overline{) \, \star \; \star \; \star} \quad \text{(quotient } 5 \, \star)$$

```
(d)          ★ 4 ★           (e)         9 ★            (f)            5 ★
        7 ) ★  9  ★                6 ) ★ ★ 2                  ★ 2 ) ★ ★ ★
                                                                     ★ ★
                                                                   _____
                                                                     ★ ★
                                                                     8 ★
                                                                   _____
                                                                       0
```

9. Solve these problems.

   (a) If $144 \times 7 = 1008$, then $14 \times 144 =$ _____

   (b) If $3 \times 314 = 942$, then $12 \times 314 =$ _____

   (c) If $25 \times 25 = 625$, then $150 \times 25 =$ _____

   (d) Find the pattern of the following and write the next two number sentences.

$$37 \times 3 = 111$$
$$37 \times 6 = 222$$
$$37 \times 9 = 333$$

   _____

   _____

   (e) 12 jars contain 96 cookies. How many cookies are there in 144 such jars?

   (f) 840 tomatoes are packed into 35 bags. How many tomatoes are there in 140 bags?

10. Find the sums of the following numbers.

    Example:

$$1 + 2 + 3 + 4 + 5 + 6 + 7 + 8 + 9 + 10$$

    Using number bonds: $1 + 10 = 11$
    $2 + 9 = 11$ and so on
    Sum of numbers from 1 to 10 $= 5 \times 11 = 55$

(a) 1 , 2 , 3 , ... 20

(b) 1 to 100

(c) 11 + 22 + 33 + 44 + 55 + 66 + 77 + 88 + 99

(d) 2 + 4 + 6 + 8 + 10 + ... + 94 + 96 + 98 + 100

(e) 1 + 3 + 5 + 7 + 9 + ... + 95 + 97 + 99

WORD PROBLEMS

1. A typist can type 495 words in 15 minutes. How many words can she type in 25 minutes?

2. Mrs. Lim baked 256 cookies on Monday. She baked 76 fewer cookies on Monday than on Sunday. If she were to pack the cookies baked on the two days into boxes of 30, how many more cookies would she need to fill up the last box?

3. Mr. Terence had 18 boxes containing 36 donuts each. He sold 162 donuts and repacked the rest into 81 boxes. How many donuts did he put into each box?

4. Elizabeth takes 35 days to write a book consisting of 630 pages.
    (a) If she writes the same number of pages each day, how many pages does she write in a day?
    (b) If Elizabeth writes another book consisting of 810 pages at the same pace, how many days will she take to complete it?

5. 500 cookies were shared equally among 25 boys and 13 girls.
    (a) How many cookies did each child get?
    (b) How many cookies were left?

6. Penny has 267 stamps in her album. Rohana has 8 times as many stamps as Penny. The number of stamps Rohana has is 12 times that of Sabrina's. How many stamps do they have altogether?

7. A worker can carry a maximum of 16 books to the storeroom at one time. 6 boxes containing 58 books each need to be taken to the storeroom. How many trips does the worker need to make altogether?

8. A crate contained 852 fruits. Each time Mr. Curly took 4 fruits from the crate, Mr. Moe took 8 fruits from it. This process of taking the fruits from the crate continued for some time. After Mr. Moe had taken 8 fruits from the crate for the last time, they found that there were no more fruits left in the crate. How many fruits did Mr. Moe take from the crate in all?

9. In a theater, there are 45 rows with 25 seats in each row. Seats in the first 5 rows are priced at $75 each and those in the remaining rows were priced at $25 each. Children are charged half the price. If the theater is full and 10 seats in the first 5 rows and 300 of the seats in the remaining rows are occupied by children, what will be the total amount of money collected?

10. A shopkeeper had 20 kg of brown rice that he packed into 200-gram and 400-gram bags. He had twice as many 400-gram bags as 200-gram bags. How many bags of brown rice did he have?

11. Mr. Shoppe bought 17 dozen of shirts for $2754. He had to throw away 24 shirts as they were torn. How much must he sell for each shirt so that he will not make any loss?

12. (a) At a sale, Jerry paid $42 for 2 tank tops and 3 T-shirts. One T-shirt costs 4 times as much as a tank top. How much did he pay for a T-shirt?
    (b) Maisy brought just enough money to buy 12 dresses. However, she only bought 9 of such dresses and had $87 left. Find the price of each dress.

13. Mr. Black earned $2 for each box of fruits he sold. He also received an extra $5 from his agent for every 15 boxes of fruits sold. How much money would he earn if he sold
    (a) 105 boxes of fruits,
    (b) 185 boxes of fruits?

14. Mrs. Quek earns $2 for each racket she sold. She earns a commission of $12 for every 25 rackets sold. How many rackets must she sell in order to earn
    (a) $248,
    (b) $506?

15. 6 similar cases of milk weigh 5430 g. Each case is packed with a dozen cartons of milk. 2 half-packed cases weigh 1290 g.
    (a) How heavy is the dozen cartons of milk? (without the case).
    (b) How heavy is an empty case?

Take the Challenge!

1. A census worker came to a house where a man lived with his three daughters. He asked the man for the age of his three daughters. The man told him that **the product of their ages is 72,** while **the sum of their ages is his house number**.

   The interviewer replied that the information given was insufficient for him to know the ages. The man then simply answered, "**The eldest loves chocolates**."

   What are the daughters' ages?

   (Hint: Make a list to explore the various possibilities.)

2. (a) A printer uses 300 digits to number the pages of a book. How many pages are there in the book?

   (b) If there are 415 pages in a second book, how many digits does the printer need to use to print the page numbers?

   (Each book is numbered from page 1.)

Topic 3: Fractions

1. Express each of the following as a mixed number in its simplest form.

   (a) $7 \div 3 =$ (b) $15 \div 4 =$

   (c) $11 \div 5 =$ (d) $28 \div 6 =$

   (e) $40 \div 9 =$ (f) $36 \div 8 =$

   (g) $\dfrac{7}{4} =$ (h) $\dfrac{14}{6} =$

   (i) $\dfrac{26}{5} =$ (j) $\dfrac{73}{6} =$

   (k) $\dfrac{34}{10} =$ (l) $\dfrac{143}{7} =$

2. Work out these problems. Give each answer as a whole number or fraction in its simplest form.

   (a) 4 children share 8 candles. How many candles does each child receive?

   (b) An apple pie was shared equally among 4 girls. What fraction of the apple pie did each girl get?

   (c) 13 boys bought and shared 5 pizzas. What fraction of a pizza did each boy get?

   (d) Mazura cuts a 12-meter string into 8 equal pieces. What is the length of each piece of string?

   (e) A bag of sugar weighing 5 kilograms was divided equally into 8 bowls. What was the weight of sugar in each bowl?

   (f) Mrs. Green poured the milk from two 1-liter cartons into 6 glasses. How much milk was there in each glass? Give your answer in liters.

   (g) A long ladder 11 yd long is 4 times as high as a fire-engine. How high is the fire-engine?

3. Add. Give each answer in its simplest form.

   (a) $\dfrac{1}{4} + \dfrac{5}{12} =$ (b) $\dfrac{7}{12} + \dfrac{2}{3} =$

(c) $\dfrac{4}{5} + \dfrac{7}{10} =$

(d) $\dfrac{3}{4} + \dfrac{5}{6} =$

(e) $\dfrac{7}{8} + \dfrac{3}{10} =$

(f) $\dfrac{7}{12} + \dfrac{5}{6} =$

(g) $\dfrac{5}{6} + \dfrac{3}{8} =$

(h) $\dfrac{3}{8} + \dfrac{2}{5} =$

4. Subtract. Give each answer in its simplest form.

(a) $\dfrac{1}{3} - \dfrac{2}{9} =$

(b) $\dfrac{3}{8} - \dfrac{1}{12} =$

(c) $\dfrac{5}{6} - \dfrac{4}{9} =$

(d) $\dfrac{3}{4} - \dfrac{1}{6} =$

(e) $\dfrac{7}{12} - \dfrac{1}{3} =$

(f) $1\dfrac{1}{3} - \dfrac{1}{2} =$

(g) $1\dfrac{5}{6} - \dfrac{9}{10} =$

(h) $1\dfrac{3}{8} - \dfrac{7}{12} =$

5. Add. Give each answer in its simplest form.

(a) $2\dfrac{3}{4} + \dfrac{1}{12} =$

(b) $1\dfrac{1}{5} + \dfrac{7}{10} =$

(c) $2\dfrac{7}{12} + 1\dfrac{2}{3} =$

(d) $1\dfrac{7}{8} + 2\dfrac{1}{2} =$

(e) $2\dfrac{7}{9} + 2\dfrac{1}{3} =$

(f) $3\dfrac{1}{6} + 2\dfrac{3}{10} =$

(g) $3\dfrac{7}{10} + 3\dfrac{5}{6} =$

(h) $2\dfrac{3}{4} + 2\dfrac{2}{5} =$

6. Subtract. Give each answer in its simplest form.

(a) $3\dfrac{7}{10} - 1\dfrac{2}{5} =$

(b) $2\dfrac{7}{9} - 1\dfrac{1}{3} =$

(c) $3\dfrac{7}{8} - 2\dfrac{1}{4} =$

(d) $4\dfrac{1}{6} - 2\dfrac{3}{4} =$

(e) $5\dfrac{1}{4} - 3\dfrac{1}{2} =$

(f) $4\dfrac{5}{6} - 1\dfrac{1}{3} =$

(g) $4\dfrac{7}{10} - 3\dfrac{1}{2} =$

(h) $3\dfrac{5}{8} - 1\dfrac{1}{6} =$

7. Work out these problems.

(a) Rosie spent $\frac{3}{8}$ of her money on a meal, $\frac{1}{4}$ of it on a movie ticket and saved the rest. What fraction of her money did she save?

(b) A waitress works $1\frac{3}{4}$ hours less in the afternoon than in the evening. If she works $5\frac{1}{3}$ hours in the afternoon, how many hours does she work in the evening?

(c) Mr. Lee gave $\frac{4}{9}$ of his salary to his wife and spent $\frac{1}{3}$ of it on a watch. What fraction of his salary was left?

(d) John is $\frac{1}{8}$ m shorter than Paul and Paul is $\frac{1}{4}$ m taller than Andrew. If John's height is $1\frac{2}{3}$ m, what is the height of Andrew?

(e) The time allotted for a Mathematics test was $2\frac{1}{4}$ hours. Annie completed the test $\frac{2}{3}$ of an hour earlier. How long did she take to complete the test?

(f) $\frac{1}{5}$ of the passengers on a bus are young adults and $\frac{2}{3}$ of them are children. The remaining passengers are senior citizens. What fraction of the passengers are not senior citizens?

(g) A flight of stairs is $10\frac{1}{3}$ m high. Jimmy walks down the stairs and still has $6\frac{5}{8}$ m of stairs to go before he reaches the bottom of the flight of stairs. How far down has he walked?

(h) Emelia mixed $3\frac{1}{4}$ liters of fruit juice with $2\frac{3}{5}$ liters of ice-cream soda to make fruit punch. How much fruit punch did she mix?

8. Find the equivalent measures.

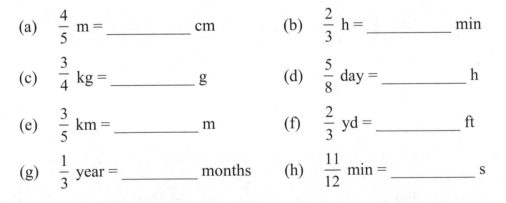

(a) $\frac{4}{5}$ m = _____ cm

(b) $\frac{2}{3}$ h = _____ min

(c) $\frac{3}{4}$ kg = _____ g

(d) $\frac{5}{8}$ day = _____ h

(e) $\frac{3}{5}$ km = _____ m

(f) $\frac{2}{3}$ yd = _____ ft

(g) $\frac{1}{3}$ year = _____ months

(h) $\frac{11}{12}$ min = _____ s

9. Give the answers in compound units.

(a) $3\frac{1}{8}$ km = _____ km _____ m

(b) $4\frac{1}{4}$ ft = _____ ft _____ in.

(c) $1\dfrac{3}{8}$ lb = _____ lb _____ oz

(d) $5\dfrac{3}{4}$ h = _____ h _____ min

(e) $2\dfrac{1}{6}$ years = _____ years _____ months

(f) $6\dfrac{9}{10}$ min = _____ min _____ s

(g) $7\dfrac{5}{12}$ days = _____ days _____ h

(h) $3\dfrac{1}{2}$ gal = _____ gal _____ qt

10. (a)   Which has a larger capacity, $3\dfrac{1}{8}$ ℓ or 3250 ml?   _____

(b)   Which is heavier, $2\dfrac{7}{8}$ kg or 2650 g?   _____

(c)   Which is shorter, $1\dfrac{2}{3}$ days or 42 h?   _____

(d)   Clarissa practices her violin for 45 minutes.

Her friend practices for $\dfrac{2}{3}$ h. Who practices
for a longer time?   _____

11. Fill in the blanks.

(a)   Express 375 ml as a fraction of 1 liter.   _____

(b)   Express 450 m as a fraction of 1 km.   _____

(c)   Express 175 cm as a fraction of 3 m.   _____

(d)   Express 55 minutes as a fraction of 2 hours.   _____

(e)   What fraction of $4 is 60 cents?   _____

(f)   What fraction of 1 ft is 10 in.?   _____

(g)   What fraction of $2\dfrac{2}{5}$ kg is 75 g?   _____

12. Work out these problems.

    (a)   In a class test, 45 out of 60 students passed.
        (i)   What fraction of the class passed?
        (ii)   What fraction of the class failed?

    (b)   Mary earned $400 a week. She saved $48 a week and spent the rest.
        (i)   What fraction of her earnings did she save each week?
        (ii)   What fraction of her earnings did she spend each week?

    (c)   Victor had 120 marbles. He lost 48 of them.
        (i)   Express the number of marbles lost as a fraction of the number of marbles he had at first.
        (ii)   What fraction of his marbles did he have left?

13. Multiply.

    (a) $\dfrac{1}{15} \times \dfrac{6}{7} =$ (b) $\dfrac{2}{3} \times \dfrac{1}{8} =$

    (c) $\dfrac{9}{10} \times \dfrac{8}{15} =$ (d) $\dfrac{3}{4} \times \dfrac{5}{9} =$

    (e) $\dfrac{9}{2} \times \dfrac{8}{3} =$ (f) $\dfrac{3}{8} \times \dfrac{16}{27} =$

    (g) $\dfrac{21}{6} \times \dfrac{18}{7} =$ (h) $\dfrac{11}{12} \times \dfrac{4}{5} =$

    (i) $\dfrac{10}{11} \times \dfrac{3}{5} =$ (j) $\dfrac{12}{15} \times \dfrac{15}{4} =$

14. Find the value of

    (a) $\dfrac{5}{6}$ of $\dfrac{9}{10}$ kg   (b) $\dfrac{1}{3}$ of $\dfrac{12}{15}$ m

    (c) $\dfrac{4}{15}$ of $\dfrac{3}{8}$ h   (d) $\dfrac{1}{2}$ of $\dfrac{5}{8}$ ℓ

15. Work out these problems.

(a) The length of a rectangle is $\frac{2}{5}$ m. Its width is $\frac{1}{2}$ m. Find the area of the rectangle.

(b) A jug contained $\frac{3}{4}$ qt of lemonade. Lily drank $\frac{4}{5}$ of it. How much lemonade did she drink?

(c) Grandma had $\frac{5}{8}$ kg of sugar. She used $\frac{3}{8}$ of the sugar to make jelly. How much sugar did Grandma use, in kg?

(d) Samuel traveled $\frac{7}{12}$ km from home to the library. He walked $\frac{5}{7}$ of the journey and ran the rest of it. How far did he run?

16. Find the value of each of the following in its simplest form.

(a) $\frac{5}{7} \div 5 = \frac{\cancel{5}}{7} \times \frac{1}{\cancel{5}} =$

(b) $\frac{2}{3} \div 4 =$

(c) $\frac{15}{6} \div 5 =$

(d) $\frac{3}{4} \div 10 =$

(e) $\frac{12}{17} \div 8 =$

(f) $\frac{3}{8} \div 2 =$

(g) $\frac{7}{8} \div 21 =$

(h) $\frac{24}{25} \div 3 =$

(i) $\frac{11}{12} \div 33 =$

(j) $\frac{2}{5} \div 3 =$

17. Work out these problems.

(a) Andy poured $\frac{3}{4}$ liter of lemon juice equally into 3 glasses. How much lemon juice was there in each glass?

33

(b) A piece of string of length $\frac{5}{6}$ m is cut into 15 shorter pieces of equal length. Find the length of each shorter piece of string.

(c) Melvin used $\frac{3}{5}$ of the soil in a bag to fill 7 pots equally. What fraction of the bag of soil did each pot contain?

(d) Sixteen similar boxes of cookies weigh $\frac{8}{9}$ lb. How heavy is each box of cookies?

(e) Michael ate $\frac{3}{8}$ of a pizza. He divided the remaining pizza into 6 equal slices and gave one slice to his friend. What fraction of the pizza did his friend have?

WORD PROBLEMS

1. Alice used $1\frac{3}{5}$ m from a roll of ribbon to tie 10 Christmas presents. What is the length of ribbon used for each present, in centimeters?

2. Anthony received $168 from his father. He saved $\frac{5}{6}$ of the money in the bank and spent the rest. How much money did he save?

3. Mariam had 441 stamps. She lost $\frac{3}{7}$ of them. How many stamps did she have left?

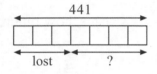

4. Sue had $3500 in her bank account. She withdrew $\frac{4}{7}$ of the money and donated $\frac{1}{4}$ of this to charity. How much money did she donate to charity?

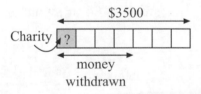

5. Mr. Magoo spent $\frac{1}{2}$ of his money on a stereo set and $\frac{1}{3}$ of his money on a television set. He then had $400 left. How much did he pay for the television set?

6. Denise bought a box of 560 pieces of candy. $\frac{4}{5}$ of the pieces of candy were fruity and $\frac{1}{4}$ of the remaining pieces of candy were mint. How many pieces of candy of other flavors were there?

7. Kenny is $1\frac{1}{2}$ times as heavy as his sister. If Kenny is 14 kg heavier than his sister, how much does Kenny weigh?

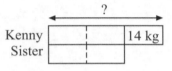

8. The length of a string is $1\frac{1}{3}$ times the length of a stick. If the length of the string is 64 in., what is the length of the stick?

9. Mimi had 126 stickers. She gave $\frac{2}{9}$ of them to her neighbor and 35 stickers to her brother. What fraction of the stickers did she have left?

10. $\frac{5}{12}$ of the guests at a party were female. There were 30 more male than female guests. Find the total number of guests at the party.

11. Ben had 50 more coins than Joan. After Joan had given 29 of her coins to Ben, she had $\frac{1}{3}$ as many coins as Ben. How many coins did Ben have at first?

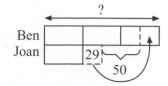

12. 889 kindergarten kids participated in a drawing contest at a park. They were divided into two groups. $\frac{1}{3}$ of the girls and $\frac{1}{2}$ of the boys were in group A. There was an equal number of boys and girls in group B. Find the number of girls and the number of boys who participated in the drawing contest.

13. Mr. Tay had 20 female carps and 5 male carps in his pond.
    (a) What fraction of the carps were male?
    (b) Mr. Tay's father brought home some male carps and put them into the pond. Then he found that $\frac{1}{5}$ of the carps were female. How many male carps did his father put into the pond?

14. $\frac{3}{4}$ of the students who join a swimming club are boys. $\frac{4}{5}$ of the girls in the swimming club are under 10 years old while 5 girls are over 10 years old.

    (a) How many girls are there in the club?

    (b) If $\frac{1}{5}$ of the boys leave the swimming club, how many students will be left in the club?

15. Lisa used 880 g of a container of sugar to bake a cake and $\frac{1}{10}$ of the remaining sugar to make cookies. She then had $\frac{3}{7}$ of the container of sugar left. How much sugar was in the container at first?

Take the Challenge!

1. Dorothy lives on Spring Street. Some new friends wanted to visit her at home but they did not know her house number. She gave a little puzzle to help them find her house number. See if you can solve the puzzle below and work out Dorothy's house number on Spring Street.

   The sum of half the number, one-third of the number and one-quarter of the number is 221.

2. In a certain village, $\frac{2}{3}$ of the men married $\frac{3}{5}$ of the women. What fraction of the population in the village are married?

   (Assume marriage of 1 male to 1 female, and no one is married to anyone living outside the village.)

3. Spring will be here soon and I want to plant some flowers in my garden where the length is longer than the width by 1 m.

   $\frac{1}{3}$ of the garden will be planted with Sunflowers,

   $\frac{1}{4}$ of the garden will be planted with Brown-Eyed Susans,

   $\frac{1}{5}$ of the garden is to be planted with Columbine,

   1 m^2 of the garden is to be planted with Foxglove

   and the last $\frac{1}{6}$ of the garden with Geraniums.

   Can you help me work out the length and width of my garden?

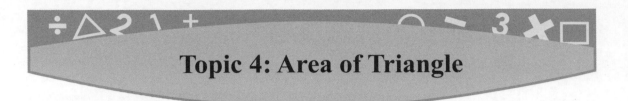

Topic 4: Area of Triangle

1. Use a set-square to draw a line to show the corresponding height (h) to the given base (b) of each triangle. The first one has been done for you.

Remember that the base and the corresponding height of a triangle must be perpendicular to each other.

(a)

(b)

(c)

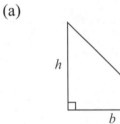

(d)

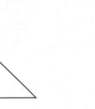

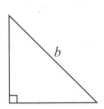

(e)

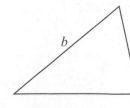

(f)

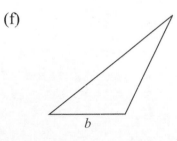

(g)

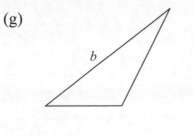

(h)

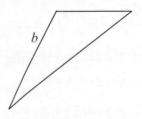

2. Fill in the blanks.
   (The symbol Δ stands for 'triangle'.)

   Example:

   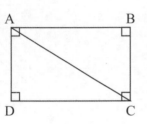

   Area of ΔACD

   $= \dfrac{1}{2} \times$ Area of Rectangle ABCD

   The area of a triangle is half the area of the related rectangle.

   (a)

   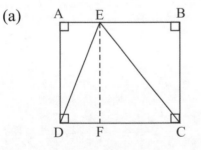

   Area of ΔDEF

   $= \dfrac{1}{2} \times$ Area of Rectangle _____

   Area of ΔECF

   $= \dfrac{1}{2} \times$ Area of Rectangle _____

   Hence,

   Area of ΔDCE

   $= \dfrac{1}{2} \times$ Area of Rectangle

   (b)

   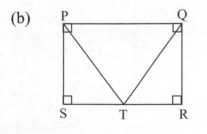

   Area of ΔPQT

   $= \dfrac{1}{2} \times$ Area of Rectangle _____

   $=$ Area of Δ _____ + Area of Δ _____

41

(c) Area of ΔTVR

= Area of Δ _____ + Area of Δ _____

Hence,

Area of ΔTVR

$= \dfrac{1}{2}$ × Area of Rectangle _____ $+ \dfrac{1}{2}$ × Area of Rectangle _____

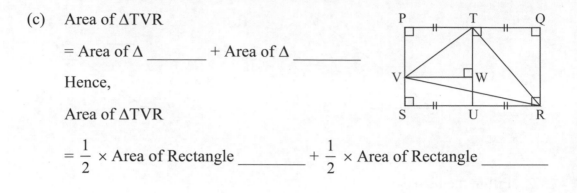

(d) ΔACE is formed by 2 smaller triangles.

Hence,

Area of ΔBCE

= Area of Δ _____ − Area of Δ _____

(e)

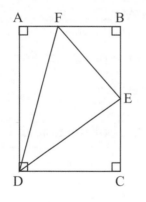

Rectangle ABCD is made up of 4 triangles.

Hence,

Area of ΔDEF

= Area of rectangle ABCD − Area of Δ _____ − Area of Δ _____

 − Area of Δ _____

3. Find the area of each of the following triangles.
   The grid is made up of 1-cm squares.

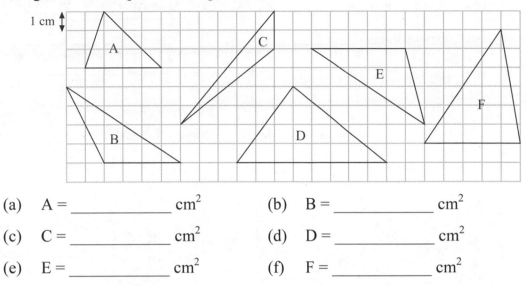

(a) A = _____ cm^2 (b) B = _____ cm^2

(c) C = _____ cm^2 (d) D = _____ cm^2

(e) E = _____ cm^2 (f) F = _____ cm^2

4. Find the area of each of the following composite figures.
   (You may look for the basic shapes like squares, rectangles and triangles that make up these figures.)
   The grid is made up of 1-cm squares.

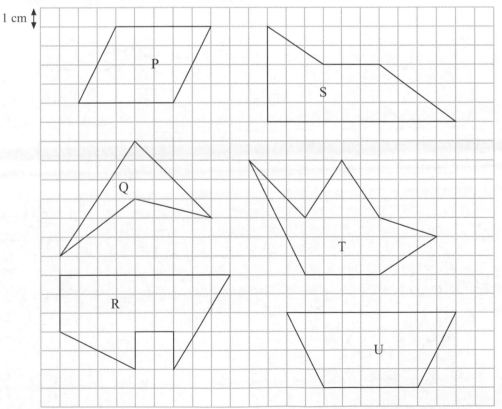

43

(a)   Area of P = _____   (b)   Area of Q = _____

(c)   Area of R = _____   (d)   Area of S = _____

(e)   Area of T = _____   (f)   Area of U = _____

5.   Find the area of each triangle.

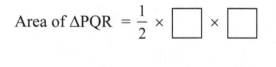

(a)

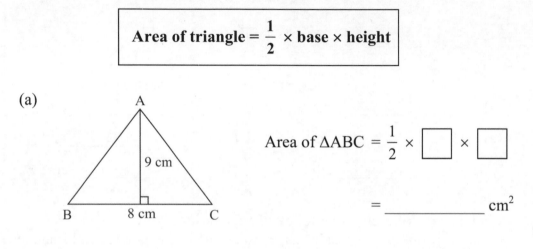

Area of △ABC = $\frac{1}{2}$ × ☐ × ☐

= _____ cm²

(b)

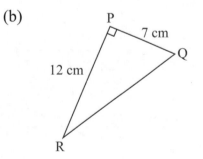

Area of △PQR = $\frac{1}{2}$ × ☐ × ☐

= _____ cm²

(c)

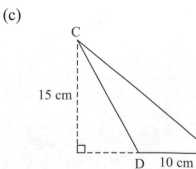

Area of △CDE = $\frac{1}{2}$ × ☐ × ☐

= _____ cm²

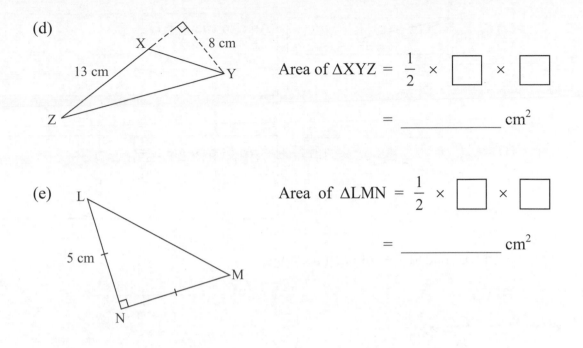

(d)

X   8 cm

13 cm   Y

Z

Area of ΔXYZ = $\dfrac{1}{2}$ × ☐ × ☐

= _____ cm^2

(e)

L

5 cm

M

N

Area of ΔLMN = $\dfrac{1}{2}$ × ☐ × ☐

= _____ cm^2

6. Find the shaded area of each rectangle.

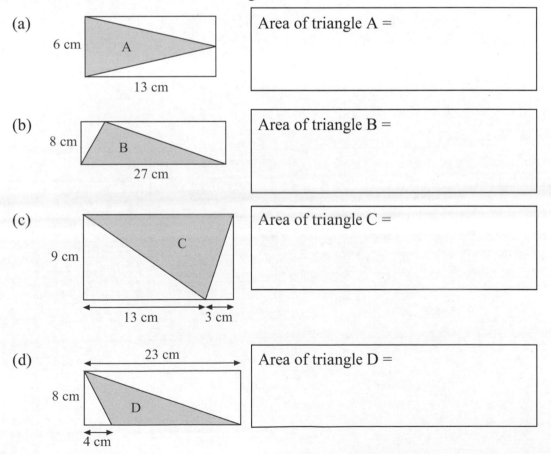

(a)

6 cm   A

13 cm

Area of triangle A =

(b)

8 cm   B

27 cm

Area of triangle B =

(c)

9 cm   C

13 cm   3 cm

Area of triangle C =

(d)

23 cm

8 cm   D

4 cm

Area of triangle D =

45

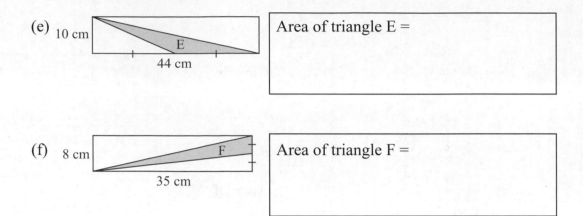

(e) 10 cm | Area of triangle E =

44 cm

(f) 8 cm | Area of triangle F =

35 cm

7. Find the shaded area of each rectangle.

(a)

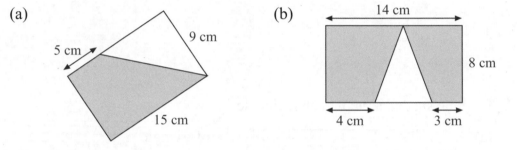

5 cm

9 cm

15 cm

(b)

14 cm

8 cm

4 cm   3 cm

(c)

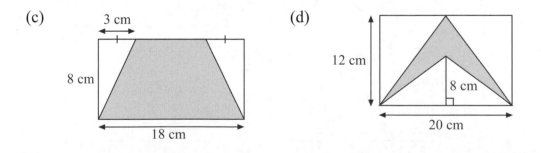

3 cm

8 cm

18 cm

(d)

12 cm

8 cm

20 cm

46

(e)
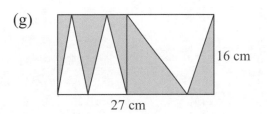
24 cm

12 cm

8 cm

10 cm

(f)
14 cm

28 cm

(g)
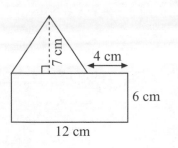
16 cm

27 cm

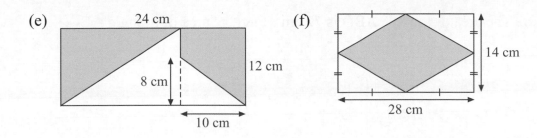

1. The figure is made up of a triangle and a rectangle.
   What is the area of the whole figure?

7 cm

4 cm

6 cm

12 cm

2. The area of triangle ABD is 72 cm². Find the area of triangle ABC.

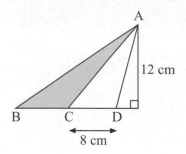

3. Find the shaded area of the rectangle.

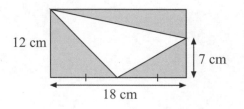

4. The right-angled triangle below is $\frac{7}{10}$ shaded. What is the area of the un-shaded part?

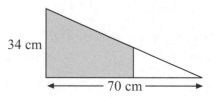

5. Find the area of figure ABCD which is formed by two triangles.

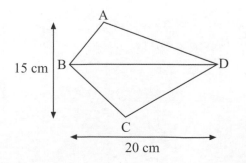

48

6. In the figure, PQRS is a square. The length of RS is 4 times as long as ST.
    (a)   What fraction of the square PQRS is the shaded triangle?
    (b)   If ST = 2 m, find the area of the unshaded square.

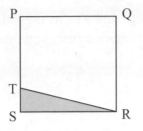

7. The figure shows a rectangular piece of paper ABCD. The paper is folded along the dotted line AE where BE = EC so that the corner B now occupies the position F. Find
    (a)   the shaded area,
    (b)   the perimeter of the shaded part.

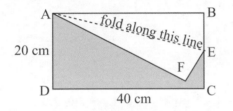

8. The figure shows two identical squares of sides 20 cm overlapping each other.
    (a)   Find the area of the overlapping part.
    (b)   Find the perimeter of the figure.

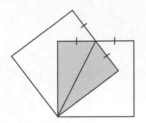

1. A square ABCD has an area of 38 cm². E, F, G and H are the mid-points of the sides. EFGH is a smaller square formed inside the square ABCD as shown. What is the area of the square EFGH?

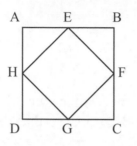

2. Find the area of each of the following figures.
    (a) A kite with diagonals 24 cm and 48 cm.

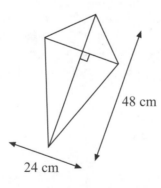

48 cm

24 cm

(b)   A parallelogram with a base of 37 cm and a height of 23 cm.

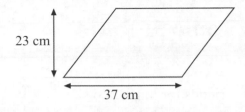

23 cm

37 cm

(c)   From the above, can you derive the formula to find the area of a kite and the area of a parallelogram?

3. The figure shows a star formed by a regular pentagon (a 5-sided polygon with equal sides) and 5 identical triangles. Each triangle has a base of 12 cm and a height of 19 cm. The perpendicular distance from the center of the pentagon to the side of the pentagon is 8.25 cm. Find the area of the star.

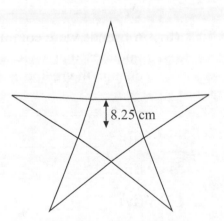

8.25 cm

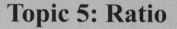
1. Weird Witch invited her friends for lunch and she decided to cook her favorite soup. This was the **recipe** for the soup serving 12 people:

   12   snake tails
   18   moldy carrots
     6   large rotten onions
     8   large green potatoes
   10   cups of pond water mixed with
         mud, salt and pepper

   Fill in the blanks.

   (a)   Following the recipe to prepare the soup for 12 people, Weird Witch needed

        (i)   _____ cups of pond water,

        (ii)   _____ large rotten onions,

        (iii)   _____ moldy carrots,

        (iv)   _____ large green potatoes,

        (v)   _____ snake tails.

   (b)   6 friends were coming for lunch. Weird Witch found that she had only 4 potatoes that were green enough to be used. She would then need to change the recipe as follows:

        (i)   _____ cups of pond water,

        (ii)   _____ large rotten onions,

        (iii)   _____ moldy carrots,

        (iv)   _____ snake tails.

   (c)   From the recipe, the ratio of the number of snake tails to the number of cups of pond water to be used is _____ : _____

2. Match the ratio to the correct drawing. The first one has been done for you.

Chairs to tables	Ratio	Drawing	Tables to chairs	Ratio	Drawing
	6 : 1	D		1 : 3	
	5 : 3			2 : 4	
	2 : 4			6 : 1	

3. Write each ratio in the simplest form.

(a) $6 : 4 =$ _____ : _____   (b) $16 : 6 =$ _____ : _____

(c) $15 : 12 =$ _____ : _____   (d) $10 : 35 =$ _____ : _____

(e) $24 : 18 =$ _____ : _____   (f) $36 : 24 =$ _____ : _____

(g) $14 : 34 =$ _____ : _____   (h) $12 : 30 =$ _____ : _____

4. In each of the following, fill in the ratio in its simplest form.

(a)

| red pens | | | | |
| blue pens | | | | |

Mr. Tan had 4 times as many blue pens as red pens. The ratio of the number of blue pens to the number of red pens is _____ : _____ .

(b)

| apples | 12 | | |
| oranges | | | |

There are 12 apples and 24 more oranges than apples. The ratio of the number of apples to the number of oranges is _____ : _____ .

(c) There are 30 blue paper clips. The number of red paper clips is 6 less than the number of blue paper clips. The ratio of the number of red paper clips to the number of blue paper clips is _____ : _____ .

(d) Clarice is 32 years old while her sister is 44 years old. The ratio of Clarice's age to her sister's age is _____ : _____ .

(e)

8 cm   6 cm

The ratio of the perimeter of the larger square to the perimeter of the smaller square is _____ : _____ .

The ratio of the area of the larger shaded triangle to the area of the smaller shaded triangle is _____ : _____ .

5. Find the ratios of the number of dotted tiles to the number of white tiles in the following figures and fill in the answers in the table below.
   (Hint: Look for a repeating pattern in which the tiles are arranged.)

   Example: Pattern A has 2 dotted tiles for every 2 white tiles
   or 1 dotted tile alternating with 1 white tile.
   Ratio = 2 : 2 or 1 : 1

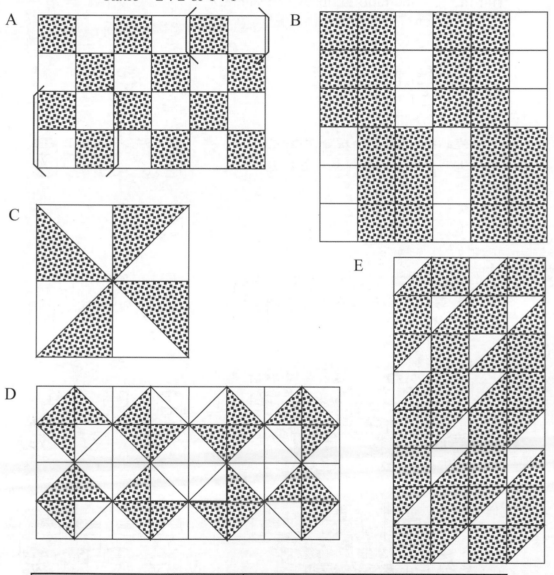

Figure	Ratio in simplest form
A	
B	
C	
D	
E	

6. Lisa wants to paint her study room with a certain shade of green which is obtained by mixing 6 cans of blue paint with 4 cans of yellow paint. This mixture of paint is not enough to paint the whole room. She has to mix more blue paint and yellow paint in the same ratio to obtain the same shade of green.

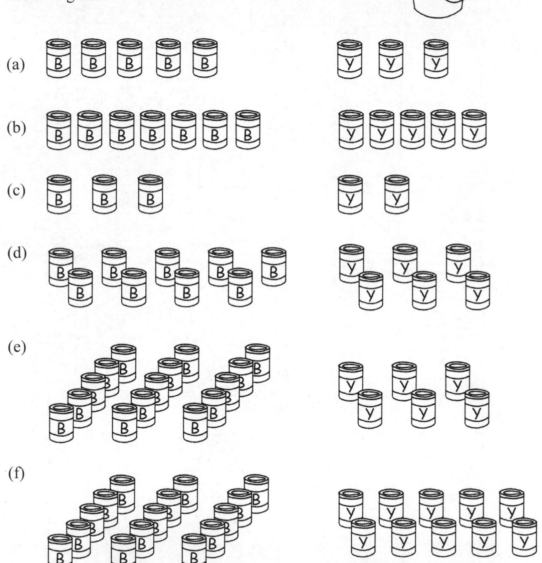

Which of the above combinations of cans of paint are in the same (equivalent) ratio as the original mixture that will give the same shade of green?
Circle all your answers.

7. Fill in the missing numbers.

(a) 5 : 3 = 20 : _____

(b) _____ : 3 = 10 : 15

(c) 6 : 15 = _____ : 5

(d) 3 : _____ = 6 : 14

(e) 24 : 3 = _____ : 9

(f) 20 : _____ = 5 : 2

(g) _____ : 56 = 2 : 7

(h) 30 : 14 = 15 : _____

8. Draw models to solve each of the following questions.

Example:
Sharon and Maria share $42 in the ratio 5 : 2.

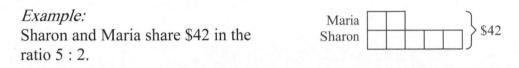

(a) The ratio of the number of swimmers to the number of non-swimmers is 4 : 1. There are 28 swimmers. How many non-swimmers are there?

(b) The length of a rectangle is three times as long as its width. The length is 6 cm longer than its width. Find the perimeter of the rectangle.

(c) A television set and a CD player weigh a total of 45 kg in the ratio 7 : 2 respectively. How much heavier is the television set than the CD player?

(d) Andy saved $\frac{1}{3}$ of his daily pocket money (that is, the ratio of the amount of his savings to the amount of his pocket money is 1 : 3). He spent $10 more than he saved. How much was Andy's daily pocket money?

(e) Aaron and John have 56 m of rope altogether. Aaron's rope is three times as long as John's rope. What is the length of Aaron's rope?

(f) The ratio of the volume of water in a glass is to the volume of water in a bowl is 4 : 5. There is 360 ml of water in the glass. How much water is in the bowl?

(g) The ratio of Davina's age to Abby's age is 3 : 5. The difference in their ages is 6 years. How old is Davina?

(h) The ratio of the number of boys to the number of girls in Primary 5K is 5 : 6. If there are 24 girls, how many students are there in Primary 5K?

(i) A sum of money is shared between 2 men in the ratio 2 : 5. If Mr. Lewis gets $750 less than Mr. Porter, what is the sum of money shared?

(j) There were 4 children to every 7 adults at a carnival. If there were 220 people at the carnival, how many children were there?

(k) 0.4 of the students in a school wear glasses. What is the ratio of the number of students who wear glasses to the number of students who do not?

9. Clara threads crystals, beads and sequins to make some bracelets and necklaces. Look at some of these designs she has made. Find the ratio of the number of beads to the number of crystals to the number of sequins used in each design and fill in the answers in the table below.
(Each diagram below shows only part of the bracelet/necklace.)

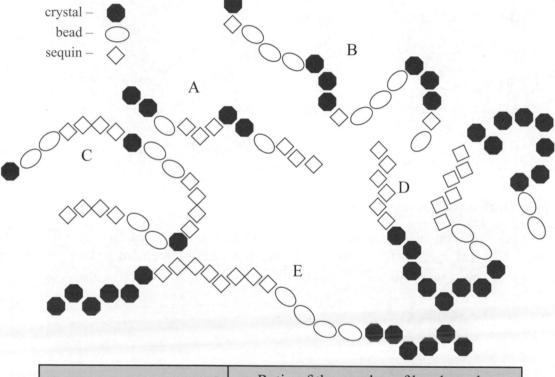

Diagram	Ratio of the number of beads to the number of crystals to the number of sequins (in simplest form)
A	
B	
C	
D	
E	

10. Write each ratio in its simplest form.

    (a) $2 : 4 : 6 =$ _____ : _____ : _____

    (b) $16 : 4 : 36 =$ _____ : _____ : _____

    (c) $42 : 30 : 12 =$ _____ : _____ : _____

    (d) $63 : 14 : 35 =$ _____ : _____ : _____

    (e) $18 : 81 : 63 =$ _____ : _____ : _____

11. Fill in the missing numbers.

    (a) $1 : 3 : 2 =$ _____ $: 6 : 4$

    (b) $2 : 5 : 10 = 4 :$ _____ $: 20$

    (c) $4 : 6 : 30 = 2 : 3 :$ _____

    (d)   _____ $: 2 : 4 = 2 : 4 : 8$

    (e) $3 :$ _____ $: 15 = : 60 : 45$

    (f)   _____ $: 5 :$ _____ $= 10 : 25 : 40$

12. Work out these problems.

    (a)   A sum of money which is more than \$10 is shared among Sally, Nora and Jane in the ratio $1 : 2 : 4$. Read each statement below and fill in each box with 'T' (True) or 'F' (False).

        Sally has \$1.

        Jane has four times as much money as Nora.

        Sally has $\frac{1}{2}$ as much money as Nora.

        Ratio of Sally's share to Jane's share is $1 : 4$.

(b) Josh is 120 cm tall, Adam is 150 cm tall and Marcus is 180 cm tall. What is the ratio of Adam's height to Josh's height to Marcus' height?

(c) The ages of Kevin, Jeremy and Colin are 42 , 63 and 49 respectively. Express the ratio of Colin's age to Jeremy's age to Kevin's age in the simplest form.

(d) Sally scored 80 points for English. For math, she scored 5 points more than English. For science, she scored 15 points less than English. What is the ratio of her English score to her math score to her science score?

(e) A string is cut into three pieces in the ratio 5 : 4 : 2. If the longest piece of string is 87 cm longer than the shortest piece of string, find the length of the string before it is being cut.

(f) Clarice is 6 years old. Dana is 14 years old. Abby is 6 years older than Dana. What is the ratio of Clarice's age to Dana's age to Abby's age in ten years' time?

(g) A bookstore sold fiction books, textbooks and workbooks last month in the ratio 6 : 5 : 9 respectively. If the store sold 1350 workbooks, what was the total number of fiction books and textbooks sold that month?

(h) What is the ratio of the area of triangle X to the area of triangle Y to the area of triangle Z in its lowest terms?

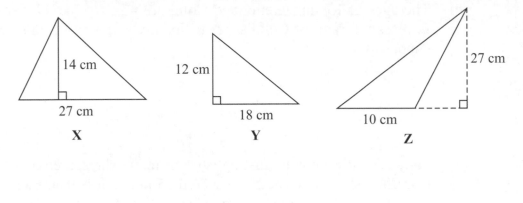

WORD PROBLEMS

1. There are 350 pigeon eggs in Mr. Eggy's stall. There are 100 fewer pigeon eggs than duck eggs. There are 500 more chicken eggs than duck eggs. Find the ratio of the number of duck eggs to the number of chicken eggs.

2. There are 40 ping-pong balls in a box. 16 of them are dented. Find the ratio of the number of dented ping-pong balls to the total number of ping-pong balls in the box if another 12 dented ping-pong balls are added into the box.

3. The total height of three friends, Sasha, Tess and Wendy, is 470 cm. The ratio of the height of Sasha to the height of Tess is 3 : 4. Wendy is 30 cm taller than Tess. Find the ratio of Tess' height to Wendy's height.

4. Josh, Ben and Rick have 70 marbles altogether. The ratio of the number of marbles Josh has to the number of marbles Rick has is 1 : 2. However, Ben has 15 marbles fewer than Rick. How many marbles does Ben have?

5. Victoria, Tim and Eliza shared a sum of money in the ratio 9 : 7 : 5. Tim and Eliza received a total of $288. How much more money did Victoria receive than Eliza?

6. Last month, the ratio of the number of boys to the number of girls in a school's computer club was 3 : 2. There were 7 more boys than girls. This month, 70 more girls join the club. What is the new ratio of boys to girls in the computer club?

7. A sum of money is shared among David, Justin and Martin.
    David's share to Justin's share is 7 : 4.
    Martin's share to Justin's share is 4 : 8.
    Martin has $750 less than David.
    What is the sum of money?

8. The ratio of the length of a rectangle to its width is 4 : 3. The perimeter of the
    rectangle is 56 cm.
    (a) How many centimeters longer is the length than the width?
    (b) What is the area of the rectangle?

9. 480 apples are sorted into 3 groups, small apples, medium-sized apples and
    big apples, in the ratio 4 : 5 : 6. The small apples are sold at 35 cents each and
    the medium-sized apples at 40 cents each. What is the price of each big apple
    if the total collection for the sale of all the apples is $204.80?

10. A piece of ribbon is cut into 3 different pieces A, B and C. The ratio of the length of A to the length of B is 3 : 4. The ratio of the length of B to that of C is 8 : 9. If C is 6 m longer than A, what is the total length of the ribbon?

11. In the figure, ABFG is a rectangle and CDEF is a square. The ratio of the length of AB to BC to CD is 4 : 1 : 2. If the area of CDEF is 36 cm², find
    (a)   the area of ABFG,
    (b)   the perimeter of the whole figure.

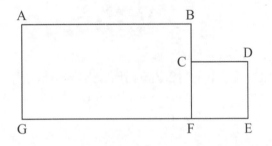

12. Mrs. Warren used $\frac{1}{2}$ of her salary to pay a loan and spent $\frac{2}{3}$ of the remainder on a refrigerator. The rest of her salary was shared among her daughter, her son and herself in the ratio 3 : 2 : 4.
    (a)   If her daughter received $120, what was Mrs. Warren's salary?
    (b)   How much did the refrigerator cost?

13. A length of rope is cut into two pieces in the ratio 7 : 9. The shorter piece is bent to form a square of side 14 cm. The longer piece is bent to form an equilateral triangle.
    (a)   What is the perimeter of the square?
    (b)   What is the length of one of the sides of the triangle?

Take the Challenge!

1. 30 men can complete a job in 12 days if each man works 8 hours a day. If the job is to be completed in 10 days with 24 men working at the same rate, how many hours must they work each day?

2. ABCD is a square with sides 9 cm. Draw three lines to divide the square into 4 triangles such that their areas are in the ratio 3 : 3 : 4 : 2.

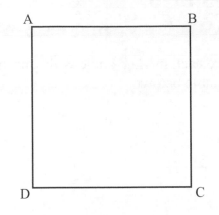

3. A ball is dropped from a height of 100 m. Each time it hits the ground, the ratio of the height it bounces up to the height from which it drops is 3 : 5. How far will the ball have traveled in the 5th bounce?

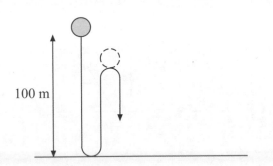

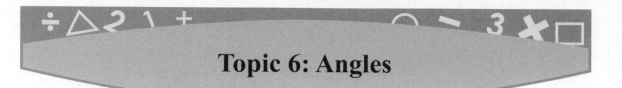

Topic 6: Angles

1. Estimate and then measure each marked angle with a protractor.
    Fill in the answers in the table below.

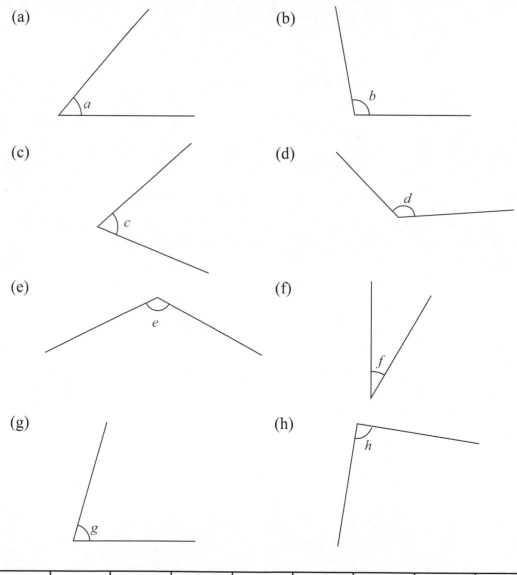

Angle	a	b	c	d	e	f	g	h
Estimate								
Measure								

68

2. Using a ruler and a protractor, draw each of the following angles.

   (a) 65°   (b) 120°

   (c) 190°   (d) 240°

   (e) 270°   (f) 320°

   (g) 335°   (h) 85°

3. Answer the questions below.

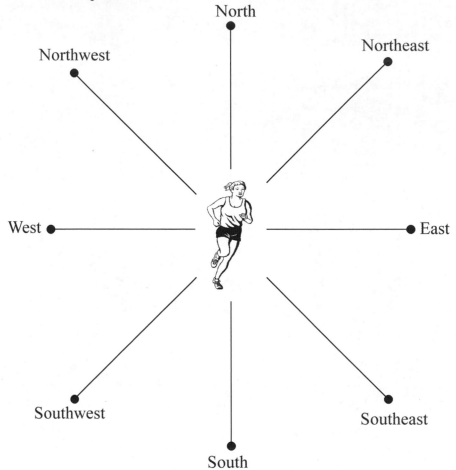

(a) The jogger is facing southeast. If she turns clockwise through 135°, which direction will she face? _____

(b) The jogger is facing west. She turns counterclockwise through 225°. Which direction is she facing? _____

(c) If the jogger faces northwest and turns to face the south, what angle has she turned through clockwise? _____

(d) If the jogger faces northeast and turns to face the northwest, what angle has she turned through counterclockwise? _____

(e) After turning clockwise through 180°, the jogger finds herself facing northeast. What direction was she facing at first? _____

(f) The jogger finally faces southwest after turning counterclockwise 315°. What direction was she facing at the start? _____

4. Using the 8-point compass, complete the story below by filling in the blanks with the correct directions.

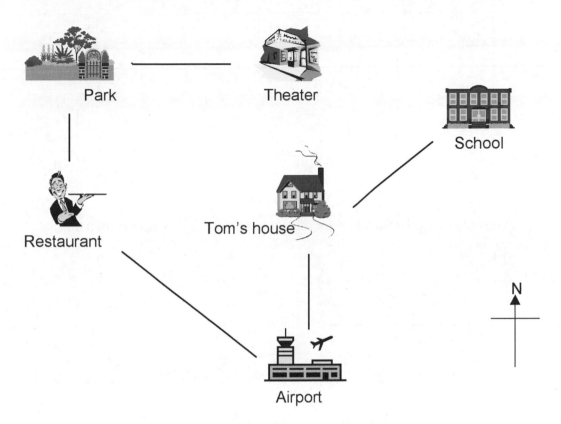

Tom woke up at 6 o'clock in the morning. He brushed his teeth, washed his face, took his breakfast and cycled _____ to school. After school, he cycled _____ back home. He took his lunch and completed his homework in the afternoon. His parents, together with him, drove _____ to the airport to pick up his aunt from Oregon. They then traveled _____ to a restaurant to have dinner together. After dinner, they took a walk in a park which is _____ of the restaurant. They finally drove _____ to a theater for a performance before going home.

5. What is the size of the angle *x* shown on the clock face?

(a)

(b)

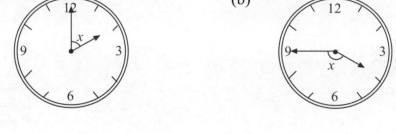

_____   _____

6. The following figures are not drawn to scale. Find the unknown angles.

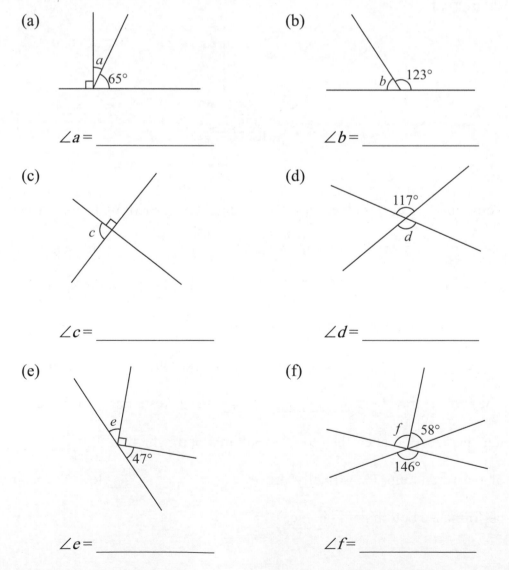

(a)

65°

∠*a* = _____

(b)

123°

∠*b* = _____

(c)

∠*c* = _____

(d)

117°

∠*d* = _____

(e)

47°

∠*e* = _____

(f)

58°

146°

∠*f* = _____

72

(g)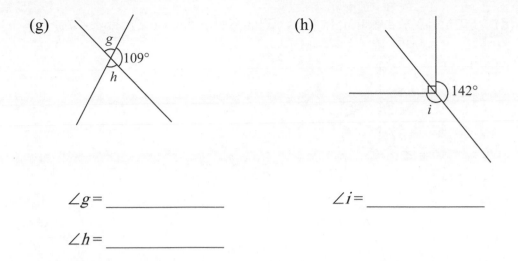

(h)

$\angle g =$ _____

$\angle i =$ _____

$\angle h =$ _____

7. The following figures are not drawn to scale. Find the unknown angles.

   (a) AB is a straight line. Find the value of angle x.

   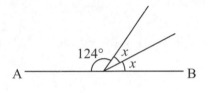

   $\angle x =$ _____

   (b) What is the value of angle z?

   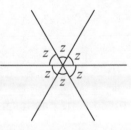

   $\angle z =$ _____

   (c) PQ is a straight line. Find $\angle p$ and $\angle q$.

   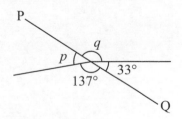

   $\angle p =$ _____

   $\angle q =$ _____

(d) ST and XY are straight lines. What is the size of ∠m and ∠n?

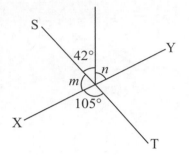

∠m = _____

∠n = _____

WORD PROBLEMS

1. In the figure, not drawn to scale, ∠x = 138°. By how much is ∠x greater than ∠y?

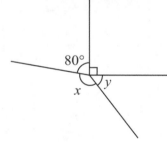

2. The figure shown is not drawn to scale. ∠x is three times as large as ∠y.
    (a) Find the value of ∠y.
    (b) How much larger is ∠x than ∠q?

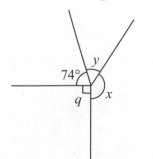

3. In the figure, not drawn to scale, AB, CD and EF are straight lines.
   (a)   Name an angle which is equal to ∠BYE.
   (b)   Find ∠CXE.

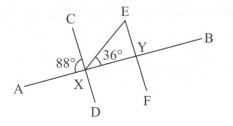

4. Look at the diagram and fill in the blanks.

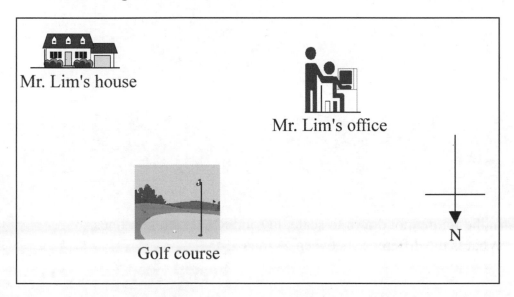

   (a)   After work, Mr. Lim went to play golf. He drove his car to the golf

         course in the _____ direction.

   (b)   Mr. Lim's house is situated _____ of the golf course.

5. In the figure, not drawn to scale, AB and CD are straight lines.
   If ∠p is three times as large as ∠r, what is the sum of ∠q and ∠r?

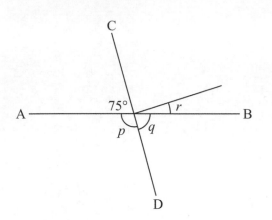

6. Measure ∠a with your protractor.
   Round off your answer to the nearest ten degrees.

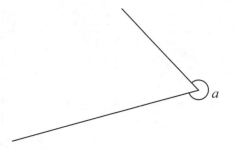

7. In the figure, not drawn to scale, PQ and RS are straight lines.
   What is the difference between ∠p and ∠q?

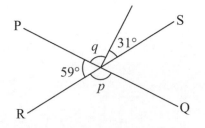

8. AC is a straight line. ∠BDE is a right angle. Find ∠ADF.

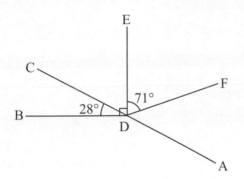

9. The figure is not drawn to scale. ST and UV are straight lines.
   Given that ∠a + ∠b = 130° and ∠b + ∠c = 95°,
   what is the value of
   (a)   ∠a,
   (b)   ∠c and
   (c)   ∠d?

10. The figure shown below is not drawn to scale. Find the value of ∠r if the ratio of ∠r to ∠s is 3 : 2.

11. WXYZ is a square. Find the ratio of ∠z to ∠x, in its simplest form.

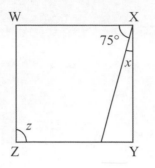

12. In the figure, not drawn to scale, ABCD is a rectangle and AC is a diagonal. The ratio of ∠a to ∠b to ∠c is 1 : 2 : 4. How much larger is ∠d than ∠ABC?

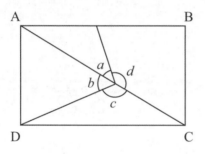

13. In the figure, not drawn to scale, AOB and COD are straight lines. Find ∠COF.

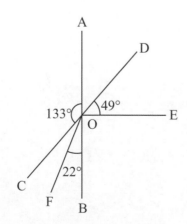

14. In the figure, not drawn to scale, PQR and SQT are straight lines.

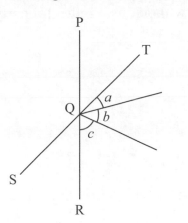

∠b is twice as large as ∠a but $\frac{2}{3}$ the size of ∠c.

If ∠c is 23° greater than ∠b, find ∠SQR.

15. A rectangular piece of paper is folded along YZ as shown. What is ∠x?

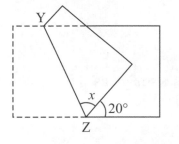

Take the **Challenge!**

1. The figure shows three straight lines.
   ∠q + ∠r = 174°.

   Which of the following statements are true? Check (✓) if the statement is true or cross (✗) if it is false.

   (a)   ∠p = ∠q   _____

   (b)   ∠p + ∠s = 180°   _____

   (c)   ∠s is greater than ∠p   _____

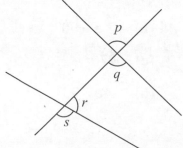

2. In each of the following figures, two rectangles overlap one another as shown. Can you explain why $\angle a = \angle b$ without using the property that vertically opposite angles are equal?

(a)

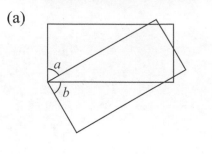

(b)

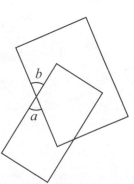

3. In the figure, a straight line XY passes through a square as shown. Which one of the following shows the correct value of $\angle d$?
   Check (✓) the correct option.

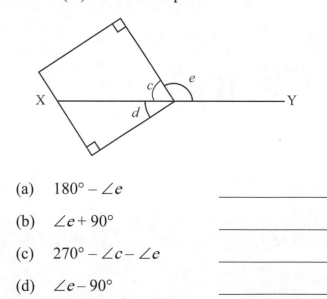

    (a) $180° - \angle e$ _____

    (b) $\angle e + 90°$ _____

    (c) $270° - \angle c - \angle e$ _____

    (d) $\angle e - 90°$ _____

Mid-Year Review

Section A

Four options are given for each question. Only one of them is correct. Choose the correct answer and write its number in the parentheses.

1. There are _____ ten thousands in the numeral 386,045.
   - (1)   6
   - (2)   8
   - (3)   38
   - (4)   86   (   )

2. The value of 5.09×1000 is _____ .
   - (1)   50.9
   - (2)   509
   - (3)   5090
   - (4)   50,900   (   )

3. In $\dfrac{3}{5} = \dfrac{3+18}{10+\square}$, the missing number in the box is _____ .
   - (1)   25
   - (2)   30
   - (3)   31
   - (4)   35   (   )

4. How many eighths are there in the sum of $2\dfrac{1}{2}$ and $1\dfrac{3}{4}$?
   - (1)   6
   - (2)   17
   - (3)   24
   - (4)   34   (   )

5. Simplify $21 + 6 \div 3 \times (11 - 4)$.
   - (1)   14
   - (2)   35
   - (3)   63
   - (4)   161   (   )

6. Which of the following is not an equivalent fraction of $\dfrac{4}{7}$?
   - (1) $\dfrac{8}{14}$
   - (2) $\dfrac{12}{21}$
   - (3) $\dfrac{20}{42}$
   - (4) $\dfrac{28}{49}$ (   )

7. The figure is made up of a square and a triangle.
   Find the perimeter of the figure if the area of the square is 64 cm².

   (1) 45 cm
   (2) 53 cm
   (3) 77 cm
   (4) 96 cm   (   )

8. It was estimated that 40,000 people attended a concert. Which one of the following is most likely to be the actual number of people?

   (1) 38,325   (2) 38,496
   (3) 39,211   (4) 39,899   (   )

9. Which one of the following is **incorrect**?

   (1) $\dfrac{1}{5}\times\dfrac{1}{5}=\dfrac{1}{25}$ (2) $\dfrac{4}{5}+\dfrac{1}{5}=1$

   (3) $\dfrac{1}{3}\times\dfrac{1}{4}=\dfrac{1}{7}$ (4) $\dfrac{1}{3}\times42=14$ (   )

10. A rectangle is 10 cm long and 15 cm wide.
    The ratio of its length to its perimeter is _____.

    (1) 2 : 5   (2) 1 : 5
    (3) 2 : 3   (4) 3 : 10   (   )

11. Grace is 9 years old and Ruth is 6 years older than Grace.
    Express Ruth's age as a fraction of their total age in the simplest form.

    (1) $\dfrac{5}{8}$ (2) $\dfrac{8}{5}$

    (3) $\dfrac{3}{5}$ (4) $\dfrac{5}{3}$ (   )

12.
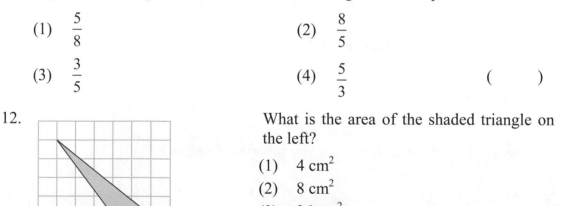

    What is the area of the shaded triangle on the left?

    (1) 4 cm²
    (2) 8 cm²
    (3) 36 cm²
    (4) 72 cm²   (   )

13. The price of a handbag to the price of a wallet is 7 : 5. If the wallet costs $12 less than the handbag, how much is the wallet?

    (1) $24   (2) $30

    (3) $42   (4) $60   (   )

14. WZ and XY are straight lines. If ∠s is three times as large as ∠t, what is the size of ∠t ?

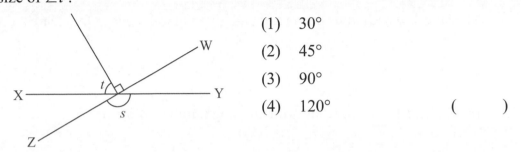

    (1)   30°

    (2)   45°

    (3)   90°

    (4)   120°   (   )

15. Mother bought $8\frac{3}{4}$ m of cloth to sew curtains. She had $1\frac{5}{6}$ m of cloth left after sewing the curtains. What was the length of cloth she used to sew curtains?

    (1) $6\frac{1}{2}$ m   (2) $6\frac{11}{12}$ m

    (3) $7\frac{1}{2}$ m   (4) $10\frac{7}{12}$ m   (   )

Section B

Write your answers in the spaces provided.
Answers must be in the units stated.

16. What is 299,513 when rounded off to the nearest thousand?

                                        Ans _____

17. How many grams are there in $4\frac{3}{10}$ kg?

                                        Ans: _____ grams

18. A face towel costs $1.90. How many face towels can Mrs. Lim buy with $17?

                                        Ans: _____ face towels

19.

Measure ∠p with your protractor and give your answer to the nearest degree.

Ans: _____ °

20. In 42 : 35 = ☐ : 5, what is the missing number in the box?

Ans: _____

21. Mrs. Whatson bought 18 apples, 24 pears and 30 oranges. What is the ratio of the number of pears to the number of oranges to the number of apples? Give your answer in its simplest form.

Ans: _____

22. Kevin left home at 7:30 am and returned at 11:05 am. How long was he away from his home?

Ans: _____ minutes

21. I am facing southwest. Which direction will I face if I turn 90° counterclockwise?

Ans: _____

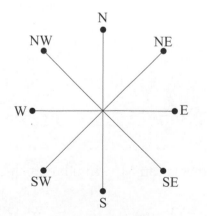

84

24. A bottle can hold 250 ml of orange juice. How many such bottles are needed to hold $4\frac{3}{5}$ liters of orange juice?

Ans: _____ bottles

25. Lily used $2\frac{7}{8}$ kg of rice to make sushi and still had $5\frac{3}{8}$ kg of rice left. How much rice did she have at first?

Ans: _____ kg

26. Paul has 42 coins and Devon has 210 coins. What is the ratio of Paul's coins to the total number of coins?

Ans: _____

27. Find the value of $\angle a$ if AB and CD are straight lines.

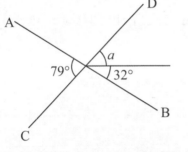

Ans: _____ °

28. Sandra and Joan shared a sum of money in the ratio 2 : 5. If Joan gave Sandra $18, they would both have the same amount of money. How much money would each of them have then?

Ans: $_____

29. Miss Tan stood on a weighing machine with 10 Primary 5 Mathematics textbooks in her hands. The scale on the weighing machine read 52.5 kg. If Miss Tan weighed 49 kg, how heavy was each textbook?

Ans: _____ grams

30. Find the perimeter of the figure.

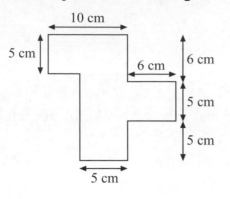

Ans: _____ cm

31. Rick read $\frac{1}{3}$ of a storybook on Sunday and $\frac{1}{6}$ of the rest on Monday. What fraction of the storybook did Rick have left to read?

Ans: _____

32. $\frac{7}{8}$ liter of lemonade is shared among 5 friends equally. How many milliliters of lemonade did each friend drink?

Ans: _____ ml

33. Some cubes are removed from solid A to get solid B. How many cubes are removed?

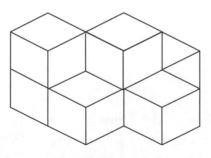

Solid A

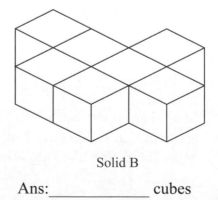

Solid B

Ans:_____ cubes

34. ABCD is a rectangle. What is the area of the shaded triangle?

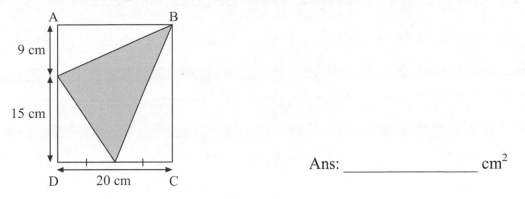

Ans: _____ cm²

35. $\frac{1}{3}$ of Tom's savings is equal to $\frac{1}{2}$ of Jane's savings. If $\frac{1}{3}$ of Tom's savings is $27, find the total savings of Tom and Jane.

Ans: $_____

Section C

For each question, show your work clearly in the space provided below it.

36. Find the value of $45 \times (36 + 14 - 3 \times 6) \div 8$.
Round off your answer to the nearest hundred.

Ans: _____

37. A triangle is drawn inside the square PQRS as shown. If the shaded part of the square is 54 cm², what is the perimeter of the square?

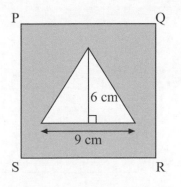

Ans: _____

87

38. Esther is $1\frac{1}{3}$ times as old as her brother. If the difference in their ages is 4 years, how old is Esther?

Ans: _____

39. A grocer bought 100 crates of mandarin oranges. Each crate contains 48 mandarin oranges. After opening the crates, he found a total of 29 spoiled oranges and he threw them away. He then packed 2500 of the good oranges into bags of four and the remaining good ones into bags of three. How many bags of oranges did he have in all?

Ans: _____

40. Emelia had $40 more than Rachel. Kimberly had $75 more than Emelia. If they had a total sum of $425, how much money did Kimberly have?

Ans: _____

41. Miss Lim ordered some flowers from a florist. $\frac{3}{8}$ of the flowers were carnations.

She ordered 54 more roses than carnations. The remaining 84 flowers were daisies. How many more roses than daisies did Miss Lim order?

Ans: _____

42. In the figure below, X and Y are squares and Z is a right-angled triangle. The ratio of the area of X to that of Y is 9 : 16. Find the area of Z if the sum of the areas of the two squares is 100 cm^2.

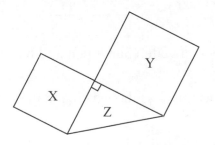

Ans: _____

43. A piece of paper is folded along the line AB as shown.
Find the ratio of ∠ABF to ∠ABE to ∠CBE in its simplest form.

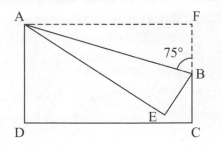

Ans: _____

44. George collected 120 more marbles than Bill. If Bill gave George 30 of his marbles, George would have three times as many marbles as Bill. How many marbles did Bill have at first?

Ans: _____

45. Sylvia saved $155. She bought a storybook, a watch and a pen and had $19 of her savings left. If the storybook cost $\frac{3}{5}$ as much as the watch and the pen cost $\frac{1}{6}$ as much as the storybook,

   (a)   what was the cost of the storybook?
   (b)   how much more did Sylvia pay for the watch than the pen?

Ans: (a) _____

(b) _____

46. Mrs. Wong bought 6 skirts and 15 blouses. Each skirt cost $2.50 more than a blouse. Mrs. Wong paid a total of $372 for all of the items.
    (a) What was the cost of a skirt?
    (b) How much money would she have saved if she had bought only 2 skirts and 3 blouses?

Ans: (a) _____

(b) _____

47. Twice as many adults as children attended a violin concert. During the intermission, 530 adults and 25 children left the concert hall. The number of children remaining in the hall became twice as many as the number of adults remaining in the hall. How many people attended the violin concert?

Ans: _____

48. (a)   As shown in the figure, points A, B, C and D are the midpoints of the
           sides of the biggest square.
           Points P, Q, R and S are the midpoints of the sides of the square ABCD.
           What fraction of the biggest square is the shaded square PQRS?

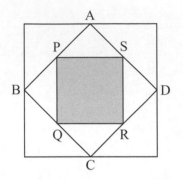

                                        Ans: (a) _____

    (b)   The figure, not drawn to scale, shows only three-quarters of a square.
           M is the midpoint of the side AB of the square.
           N is the midpoint of AM.
           What is the ratio of the shaded area to the area of the figure?

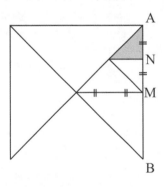

                                        Ans: (b) _____

49. Tim, Steve and Henry shared a sum of money in the ratio 2 : 7 : 5. If Steve were to spend $\frac{3}{7}$ of his money, he would have $76 left.

   (a)   How much more money had Steve than Henry?
   (b)   How much must Steve give to Tim so that they would each have the same amount of money?

Ans: (a) _____

(b) _____

50. Mr. Lee gives his wife part of his monthly salary and $\frac{1}{3}$ of the remaining money is given equally to his three children. He then has $\frac{6}{11}$ of his salary left.

   (a)   What fraction of his salary does each of his children receive?
   (b)   If Mr. Lee's wife receives a monthly allowance of $500, what is his salary?

Ans: (a) _____

(b) _____

More Challenging Problems

1. Mr. and Mrs. Keet have four children. They were born one year apart. The ages of the four children when multiplied together is 360. What is the age of the eldest child?

2. Complete the following number sentences using the four signs of operations (+, −, ×, ÷) and parentheses. The first one has been done for you.

   (a)   (4 + 4) ÷ (4 + 4)   =   1

   (b)   4   4   4   4   =   2

   (c)   4   4   4   4   =   3

   (d)   4   4   4   4   =   4

   (e)   4   4   4   4   =   5

   (f)   4   4   4   4   4   =   6

(g) 4   4   4   4   =   7

(h) 4   4   4   4   =   8

(i) 4   4   4   4   =   9

3. In each of the following, fill in the boxes with '+' or '×' signs to make the number sentence correct.

(a) 1 ☐ 2 ☐ 3 ☐ 4 ☐ 5 ☐ 6 ☐ 7 ☐ 8 ☐ 9 = 44

(b) 1 ☐ 2 ☐ 3 ☐ 4 ☐ 5 ☐ 6 ☐ 7 ☐ 8 ☐ 9 = 100

4. There are three Grade 5 classes. They are 5A, 5B and 5C.
    If one student from 5A is being transferred to 5B, there will be an equal number of students in these two classes. If one student from 5B is being transferred to 5C, there will be one student more in 5C than in 5B. Which class has more students at first, 5A or 5C? How many more students?

5. A long strip of paper is about 15 cm by 1 cm.
   (a) It is folded exactly into two along its width. It is then cut across the center of the folded piece along its width. How many pieces of paper will there be?
   (b) If the strip of paper is folded into two halves and then into two halves again from the folded piece, how many pieces of paper will there be if the final folded piece is then cut across the center along its width?

6. In a little canvas bag, there are 10 red marbles, 10 blue marbles and 10 green marbles. Without looking into the bag, Mark draws one marble from the bag each time.
   (a) At least how many times must Mark draw a marble from the bag so that he will surely obtain at least two marbles of the same color?
   (b) At least how many times must Mark draw a marble from the bag so that he will surely obtain marbles of at least two different colors?

7. In the right-angled triangle ABC, AB = AC and BC = 10 cm. Find the area of triangle ABC.

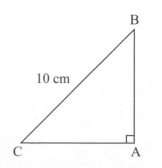

8. In the diagram, O is the center of the circle. AB and CD are the diameters of the circle. The area of the shaded part is 234 cm². Find the area of the square EFGH.

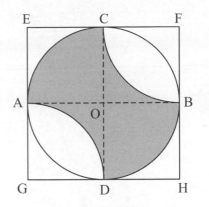

9. ABCD and EFGC are two squares as shown. The lengths of their sides are 11 cm and 9 cm. Find the area of the shaded region.

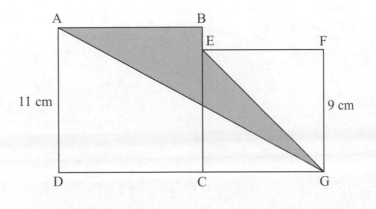

10. ABCD is a rectangle of length 18 cm and width 14 cm. E is the midpoint of BC. Find the area of the shaded triangle BEF.

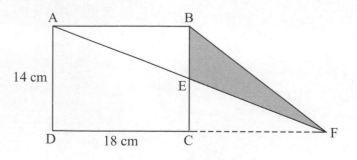

11. In the following addition, fill in the boxes with the numbers 1, 2, 3, 4, 5, 6, 7 and 8 so that the sum is 153. Each number can only be used once.

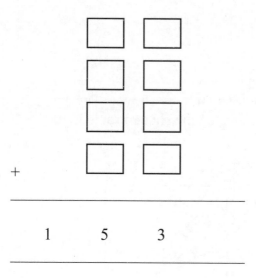

12. In the following multiplication, A, B, C and D represent different digits. What is the answer for the multiplication?

```
        A   B   C   D
    ×               D
   ─────────────────────
        D   C   B   A
   ─────────────────────
```